CDR Jim Wright, CGAS Kodiak Operations Officer- *"How powerless I felt as the helicopter inched its way up the side of the mountain in the fog, rain, and wind to the survivors. We on the C-130 vividly could imagine that the helo crew was acting more like an ATV than a rotary wing aircraft, without the benefit of wheels on the ground. This was the most complex and remote a SAR case I have ever been associated with in my 20 years in the Coast Guard. We had so many people doing selfless work...AVDET, Mellon, LORAN Station, Shemya AFB, and other CGAS Kodiak crews. Seeing the photos of wreckage and knowing how bad the weather was, I was totally astounded that we had survivors."*

CAPT Jim Sabo, CGC *Mellon* Operations Officer- *"Upon reflection on the CG-1600 operation over 30 years later, I believe there was a coming together of too many factors to be considered coincidence. Call it fate, luck, or divine intervention, but Mellon, with the personnel involved, became the right tool, at the right time, and in the right place to successfully prosecute this mission...someone was looking out for those survivors. The Coast Guard is, however, Always Ready...Semper Paratus. It is staffed with personnel who will 'always' demonstrate Honor, Respect, Devotion to Duty, and Courage."*

Sgt. Darlene J. Turner, Kodiak Post Commander, Alaska State Troopers (Retired)- *"Captain Peterson's and Captain Wallace's book, "A Miracle at Attu", is mesmerizing and a true jaw clincher... I could not walk away from it. The danger and hazards the pilots and crews face every day in Alaska would give most others pause. This book demonstrates the true passion and courage these brave men showed during a very stressful rescue. It is a chilling, gut wrenching and inspirational account of an impossible rescue. The men and women of the USCG have my utmost respect. Fantastic job Bill and Mike."*

A Miracle at ATTU: The Rescue of CG-1600
Copyright ©2016 Bill Peterson

ISBN 978-1506-902-98-2 HC/CL
ISBN 978-1506-902-87-6 PBK
ISBN 978-1506-902-88-3 EBOOK

LCCN 2016952576

September 2016

Published and Distributed by
First Edition Design Publishing, Inc.
P.O. Box 20217, Sarasota, FL 34276-3217
www.firsteditiondesignpublishing.com

Library of Congress Cataloging-in-Publication Data
Peterson, Bill
   A Miracle at ATTU: The Rescue of CG-1600/
written by Bill Peterson.
   p. cm.
   ISBN 978-1506-902-87-6 pbk, 978-1506-902-88-3 digital

1. HISTORY / Military / U.S. Coast Guard. 2. / Alaska. 3. / Aviation.

A11195

A Miracle at ATTU: The Rescue of CG-1600

By
CAPTAIN Bill Peterson (USCG ret.)
with
CAPTAIN Mike Wallace (USCG ret.)

Dedicated To the men and women of the U.S. Coast Guard- Honor, Respect, and Devotion to Duty

Preface

U. S. Coast Guard personnel have gone into harm's way to rescue and assist others for 226 years (1790-2016). In 1982 the U. S. Coast Guard responded to 68,552 search and rescue cases saving 5,675 lives.[1] This book is an historic nonfiction account documenting one of those rescues. This was a unique rescue as it involved a U. S. Coast Guard HC-130H that crashed on a logistics mission to the remote Coast Guard Long Range Navigation Station on Attu Island Alaska. The names and events described in this book were derived directly from first-hand accounts provided by Coast Guard logs, records, news releases, and interviews obtained through Freedom of Information Act requests. I used my own notes and knowledge as the rescue pilot, as well as my co-pilot's, to describe the rescue as it unfolded. I supplemented the official documents with additional survivor and rescuer interviews conducted over 30 years after the mishap. Several hundred hours of hours of research was completed to corroborate the facts presented in the book. No characters were added, no names changed, and no events fabricated.

The Coast Guard was more than a job for me, it was a "calling" and I would say for most that made it a career. It takes a special person to go into harm's way and fly into the storm so others may live. I was both honored and blessed to have served with the most dedicated and professional men and women for over 30 years (1972-2005) in the Coast Guard.

It is my hope this book serves three purposes: to describe the selfless actions of the men and women of the U. S. Coast Guard who conducted the rescue; to raise awareness of the work the Coast Guard accomplishes in service of our nation; and to help raise awareness of Coast Guard Aviation "flying into the storm" during our 100th anniversary celebration (1916-2016).

Foreword

A Miracle at Attu: The Rescue of CG-1600 is an inspiring and emotional story of human error, courage, bravery, and survival. CAPT Bill Peterson's extraordinary account of the phenomenal rescue efforts following the crash of CG-1600 in the mountains of Attu Island is gripping and emotional. CAPT Peterson's words guide the reader to feel the tension, the danger, the risk, and the determination to locate the downed C-130, as well as find and rescue all of the crewmembers and passengers.

This is a miraculous story of personal sacrifice and exceptional courage brought to us through the eyes of a young rescue pilot. He documents the heroic actions of all involved in the rescue including the surviving crewmembers. He captures the rescue effort by putting the reader right in the cockpit with him. The reader will feel how physically and psychologically draining the rescue effort was...for everyone involved.

The decision making process on board CGC *Mellon*, so vividly described, is one lesson that everyone should learn (or relearn). Having spent much of my adult life flying Coast Guard helicopters in Alaska, the detail and descriptions are incredible.

CAPT Peterson puts the entire rescue into the historical context; Attu during World War II, Alaska Native history, as well as Coast Guard aviation history.

Thank you for telling this remarkable story and for documenting an important part of Coast Guard Aviation history in Alaska.

RADM James C. Olson (USCG ret)

RADM Olson served in Alaska as Operations Officer CG Air Station Sitka, Commanding Officer CG Air Station Sitka AK, Commanding Officer CG Air Station Kodiak AK, and Commander CG District Seventeen for all of Alaska.

Chapter 1

ANSWERING THE CALL

**"Now faith is confidence in what we hope for
and assurance about what we do not see."**
Hebrews 11:1

"Bill, we have a possible downed aircraft."

Lieutenant (LT/03) Jim Sabo, Operations Officer on Coast
Guard High Endurance Cutter *Mellon* (WHEC 717), looked at us
anxiously as LT Mike (Wally) Wallace, my copilot, and I reached
the bridge of *Mellon*, responding to his urgent request. Wally and I
had had just returned from a morning law enforcement flight,
landing our HH-52 helicopter aboard the cutter's diminutive flight
deck, near Buldir Island at the western end of the Alaskan
Aleutian chain.

0940 local Friday 30 July 1982

Standing beside Sabo on the bridge by the navigational chart
on the Quartermaster's table, we heard an auto alarm on the high-
frequency radio emergency channel, 2182 kHz, followed by an
urgent safety broadcast from Coast Guard **Com**munications
Station (COMSTA) Kodiak: "PAN PAN (pause) PAN PAN (pause)
PAN PAN (pause) This is Communications Station Kodiak,
Communications Station Kodiak, A US Coast Guard HC-one thirty,
Coast Guard number one-six-zero-zero, is missing on a flight from
Shemya **A**ir **F**orce **B**ase (AFB) to Attu Alaska; any mariner in

contact with or having information on Coast Guard number one-six-zero-zero contact 'COMSTA' Kodiak immediately."
The message was repeated; no one was listening. Our minds had instantly raced to the possibility of a downed Coast Guard (CG) HC-130H and thoughts of the aircrew and shipmates that may be in danger.
I immediately told Sabo I had heard a radio transmission, from CG-1600 around 0825, stating, "Landing in ten" when we were flying our fisheries patrol. This new information was immediately relayed back to COMSTA Kodiak by *Mellon*.

0942
Coast Guard North Pacific Search and Rescue Coordinator (NORPACSARCOORD) in Juneau, Alaska, ordered *Mellon* to "proceed at best possible speed to the last known position of Coast Guard sixteen hundred".
The HC-130's last suspected position was on final approach for a landing at Casco Cove, Attu Island, Alaska. *Mellon*, with a deployed helicopter aboard, immediately diverted from its assigned Alaskan Fisheries Patrol (ALPAT) to begin the Search and Rescue (SAR) mission. The cutter's Commanding Officer (CO), Captain (CAPT/06) Martin Daniell, ordered the helmsman to come about to a westerly heading of 290 degrees and then notified the ship's crew of the situation via the shipboard public addresses system.
"*Mellon* is proceeding at best speed back to Attu; Juneau has designated *Mellon* the On-Scene Coordinator for a possible downed Coast Guard HC one thirty on its logistics flight from Shemya AFB to Attu."
Everyone on *Mellon* was on an adrenalin rush. This was "one of our own"; a Coast Guard aircraft and aircrew that were missing. For our-six man helicopter crew deployed aboard *Mellon* from Coast Guard Air Station (CGAS) Kodiak, AK, the news was even more shocking because personal friends and workmates were onboard the missing aircraft. We had just rendezvoused with the CGAS Kodiak HC-130H, CG-1600, a few days before at Attu Island to receive a new helicopter battery during the first of their many logistics sorties to resupply Coast Guard Long Range Navigation (LORAN) Station Attu.

On Wednesday 28 July at 1730 local, CG-1600 had been parked on the tarmac at the Casco Cove runway next to our HH-52A, CG-1425. CG-1600 was on a routine scheduled logistics mission to keep the remote LORAN Station running. HC-130s from Kodiak were the life line for the isolated Alaskan LORAN Stations of Attu, Port Clarence, and St. Paul. The arrival of the logistics flights was always uplifting for the station crew. The crew of CG-1600 had just flown from Kodiak to Attu with a brief stop in Adak, a distance of 1,195 nautical miles (nm) or the approximate distance from Miami, FL, to Boston, MA.

This would be one of many sorties planned for CG-1600 into Attu. CG-1600 would also fly some short fisheries enforcement flights in support of *Mellon*, depending on weather, as a bonus since they were deployed to this area. It was standard for all Coast Guard logistics flights to conduct multi-missions when operating from remote locations when possible.

I had contacted CGAS Kodiak via high-frequency radio (HF) phone patch to coordinate a new battery for us because the current helicopter battery was not maintaining its charge. My crew had already changed out batteries once, with a spare carried in the helicopter support kit (HSK); this would mean we would have a fresh spare. CG-1600 would stage from Shemya AFB with its 10,000-foot runway and facilities, only 35 nm east of Attu, on its 3-day supply and fisheries enforcement missions. It was very rare that two CGAS Kodiak-based aircraft were at Attu simultaneously. It was also very rare that the Aircraft Commander's (AC) for the HC-130 and the HH-52, LT Mark Whyte and me, were next-door neighbors at base housing in Kodiak.

On my way to the helo from the LORAN Station, I saw Mark and said hello; thanked him for bringing out the battery; and asked him to pass a message to my wife, Tina, that "All was well. We're all doing fine on the ALPAT." Mark was scheduled to get back to Kodiak on Friday 30 July, and I would be deployed another month on *Mellon* in the Bering Sea. In 1982 ALPAT AVDET deployments were for approximately 60 days and we had limited to no communication capability (e.g., no email or text messaging) while deployed to talk with our loved ones.

Mark said no problem; he'd pass the message on and for us to be safe as I climbed into CG-1425 to fly back to *Mellon*. Wally opened his cockpit window and handed Mark a letter to his wife Sharon and asked if he would deliver it. Mark replied, "I will." *Neither of us knew the message and the letter would not be passed as requested...*

Mellon was now heading toward the western flanks of Attu Island in Alaska's Aleutian chain. Daniell ordered all ahead full. The cutter's two Fairbanks-Morse diesel engines accelerated and delivered all of their 7,000 horsepower. The engines, which are a larger version of a 1968 diesel locomotive design, now propelled the 2,478-ton High-Endurance Cutter through the seas at 17 knots, but more speed was necessary.

0952
The first of two Pratt-Whitney marine gas turbines (nicknamed the "birds" because of their high-pitched whine, which was heard throughout the ship), similar to jet engines installed on Boeing 707s, was brought on line. Three minutes later, the second gas turbine was on line. Within fifteen minutes, the turbines were generating a total of 36,000 shaft horsepower, which powered the cutter's twin screws at full speed, 28 knots, heading into many unknowns.

Meanwhile LORAN Station Attu was already an hour into their overdue and possible downed aircraft procedures. The 24-man unit had initiated calls in the blind on their radios trying to raise CG-1600; they had contacted Shemya AFB and CGAS Kodiak to report CG-1600 overdue and find out if the aircraft had been diverted to another mission; and they had dispatched their two Thiokol tracked vehicles with additional personnel and medical supplies to conduct shoreline searches around Alexai Point to the northeast and Murder Point to the southwest. Mountains with no roads precluded any search to the north, and the waters of Massacre Bay and the North Pacific precluded any search to the south. A curtain of fog, dropping visibility to 100 feet, now ringed Casco Cove and the LORAN Station, impeding any visual searches of the surrounding areas. No one knew what had happened to CG-1600.

1010

Mellon was halfway between Kiska and Buldir Islands, approximately 150 nm east of Attu in position 52-31.0N 176-11.4E. *Mellon* is a Secretary Class High-Endurance Cutter. Her keel was laid on 25 July 1966 at Avondale Shipyards in New Orleans, LA. She was commissioned on 9 January 1968 and named after the 49th Secretary of the Treasury, Andrew W. Mellon. She was one of the first naval vessels built with a combined diesel and gas turbine propulsion plant. Classified as a WHEC meant she was designed to remain at sea for extended periods of time to undertake mid-ocean search and rescue operations and to conduct extended law enforcement missions. She had a range of 10,000 nm at 20 knots. She carried a crew of up to 15 officers and 149 enlisted.[2]

Daniell had all department heads and senior operations personnel assemble in the cutter's Combat Information Center (CIC) to discuss a rescue plan. Daniell had Sabo lead the planning meeting with everyone huddled around National Oceanic and Atmospheric Administration (NOAA) navigational chart 16420 (chart for Near Islands, Buldir to Attu) on CIC's tactical watch table. Wally and I listened intently as Sabo briefed.

"Weather is not good, 'Aleutian standard', and is not forecast to get any better. Visibility is variable from one-half mile to five miles in fog with light to moderate precipitation."

During the morning ALPAT sortie from *Mellon*, we had to cut our enforcement flight short because of extremely low visibility, less than one half nm, in the patrol area near Kiska Island.

"The overcast cloud layer is variable from 200 to 400 feet," Sabo continued. "Winds are blowing out of the southwest at 20 to 30 knots with higher gusts. Seawater temperature is 44 degrees, and air temperature is 44 and expected to rise to only 48 degrees later in the day. The combined seas and swells are 10 to 14 feet aligned with the wind and will remain on the bow for the entire transit until blocked by Attu Island. No break in the weather is forecast. Navigational hazards and shoal waters abound, especially near Attu, around CG-1600's final approach path into Massacre Bay, with Casco Cove at its terminus. We will require the special sea detail and navigational team for any high-speed transit from Agattu Strait into Massacre Bay due to the significant navigational hazards."

It was not the worst weather Wally and I had flown in by far, but it was not good anyway you looked at it...the good thing was it was summer and we had plenty of daylight in these northern latitudes!

Discussions finally turned to worst-case scenarios for CG-1600 and her crew. Sabo turned to me to take over that portion of the brief. Wally and I both spoke up. We voiced our concerns on the possibility CG-1600 had ditched or somehow crashed at sea on the approach. Hypothermia could kill most of the crew in less than two hours, if they had survived impacting the water and safely egressed the ditched aircraft. The HC-130 carried deployable life rafts, but what if the rafts didn't deploy as designed or the aircrew couldn't get into the rafts or survival suits they carried on board? They would be in real trouble in the 44 degree water in just their flight gear.

Wally and I knew what occurred during the annual cold water immersion training in Woman's Bay (Kodiak) held for all aircrew members at CGAS Kodiak. The helicopter crews felt the HC-130 crews took a laid back approach to the training, because they would put on their survival suits on land before entering the water. They thought that ditching would be a controlled event for the four-engine HC-130, and the crew would have time to don their survival suits before they ditched.

The helicopter crews were not allowed "this luxury" because it was felt a helicopter ditching or the more likely scenario of inadvertent contact with the water would not afford helicopter crews any time to don survival suits. Helicopter crews went into the water, during training, in only our flight gear, which in 1982 was 3/8-inch neoprene wet suits sans our flight boots, flight gloves, and flight helmets. After entering the water, we then had to get into the survival suit. In the frigid winter waters of Woman's Bay (34 to 40 degrees), this was not an easy feat. The water was so cold; it sucked the air out of your lungs when you jumped in off the dock. On initial water contact, you came up gasping for air and even with a wet suit on, you started to lose feeling and dexterity in your hands and arms immediately. You needed your hands and arms to pull on the survival suit quickly; in ten minutes or less your hands turned to stone.

If CG-1600 had ditched without warning, the crew would have had no time to don their survival suits before immersion in the 44 degree water wearing only their flight suits. Getting into a survival suit or a raft would be their only hope for survival unless a rescue helicopter could get there soon. Wally and I had extensive training on hypothermia, and we both knew body thermal conductivity in water is twenty-six times faster than when exposed to air, which means under ideal conditions, exhaustion and or unconsciousness would occur in 30 to 45 minutes, and survival time was only one to two hours at most in just a flight suit.[3]

Discussion of a crash on land ensued. Everyone knew how rugged the terrain was with mountains surrounding Casco Cove. What sort of crash was it? Could the aircrew have survived a crash into the terrain around the runway? I had several nagging questions with no answers.

Why had none of the Attu Coast Guard personnel seen or heard anything as they were manning the crash rescue vehicles at the runway for CG-1600's arrival?

If the weather was as bad as we had seen earlier on our fisheries flight and reported at Attu presently, why did CG-1600 even try to get into Attu?

What caused them to crash and where?

Did they crash, or were they flying a patrol trying to gain communications with COMSTA Kodiak or another communications station?

The logistics flight to Attu was a monthly flight to support this very remote LORAN Station. Attu Island's strategic location, at the western end of the Aleutian chain and 1,282 nm west of Anchorage, AK, was ideal for the LORAN system, which had operated on Attu since 1944. During World War II, all information about LORAN Stations was classified SECRET because the stations were used both for sea and air navigation in these remote areas by allied forces. After the war, LORAN and station locations were declassified, allowing this navigational system to be used by all mariners and pilots operating vessels and aircraft with installed receivers.

The current LORAN C Station had been operational at Casco Cove since July 1961. This was one of several remote Alaska LORAN C Stations (Attu, Port Clarence, St. Paul, and Kodiak) that provided highly accurate navigational signals from fixed land-based radio beacons for the Bering Sea and North Pacific Ocean. They were critical to the safe navigation of all mariners in those waters and for many aircraft flying in this remote region of the world.[4]

Mellon was informed two land search teams were deployed by Station Attu, and LT Sabo, who had been a previous CO of the LORAN Station in 1977, briefed us on the limited road system (20 miles) and area surrounding the approaches and runway at Casco Cove. One search team was assigned the Murder Point area, which had been the old LORAN A Station location and a prominent point to the west of Massacre Bay. Some of its buildings were still intact since it's decommissioning in 1961, but no power or facilities were operational. The other team was assigned the Alexai Point area, which had been an old World War II Navy Marsden matting runway and the most prominent point to the east of Massacre Bay.

These two points of land had been used for years by Coast Guard pilots and navigators to safely fly into Attu using radar as a backup for the visual approach. Casco Cove had no instrument approach or navigational aids to assist the pilots. Identifying and flying over Alexai Point or Murder Point provided the pilots adequate clearances from the 3,000-foot mountainous terrain, which formed a semicircle around the runway and the 625-foot LORAN tower just north of the 6,300-foot primary runway (designated runway 2-20).

All logistics flights into Casco Cove had to be flown in visual meteorological conditions (VMC). In uncontrolled airspace (e.g., Class G) like Attu's, there was little chance any other aircraft would be flying, so remaining clear of clouds and maintaining one mile visibility was all that would be required per the Federal Aviation Administration (FAA). However CGAS Kodiak Air Operations Manual set more stringent weather minimums, at 400-foot ceiling and three mile visibility to attempt a landing. With no automated weather reporting equipment installed, Station Attu personnel had reference points equating to one to three miles visibility and ceilings from 100 to 1,000 feet. Station personnel would pass their "window weather" based on the reference points to the pilots when they called before attempting a flight into Casco Cove.

LT Sabo knew the capabilities and limitations of the tracked vehicles that had been sent out by the station for the initial land search. He knew they were better than four-wheel drive vehicles, but they were no match for the boggy tundra that rendered them useless on most of the island. Many times the tracked vehicles would become mired in the tundra because the tracks would just churn and dig a hole in the wet quagmire. LT Sabo had to rescue his tracked vehicles time and again when personnel thought they could "make it" off the roads in the machines. He knew the island and how difficult it would be to rescue any survivors in that environment if the crash had occurred off the road system.

With no MAYDAY call or emergency beacon from CG-1600, *Mellon* had little to no concrete information to go on. My recommendation was that we launch Rescue-1425 with a maximum fuel load to get on-scene as quickly as possible to find the crash site, assess the situation, and hopefully rescue any survivors. Daniell agreed, but he did not feel it safe or prudent for the single-engine HH-52 helicopter to fly 150 nm over the Bering Sea in poor weather without cover and with limited options.

The HH-52 amphibious hulled helicopter designated the "Seaguard" was designed for search, rescue, and law enforcement missions by Sikorsky Aircraft. The Coast Guard purchased 99 HH-52 helicopters, which were delivered between 1963 and 1969. It was smaller than the U.S. Navy twin engine SH-3 Sea King helicopter also built in the 60s. The helicopter had a maximum speed of 109 knots forward, 20 knots rearward, and 25 knots sideward. Maximum range was 474 nm, with maximum fuel and limited operational equipment (e.g., stripped aircraft) and 250-nm range with maximum fuel ALPAT configured. The HH-52 was the mainstay for Coast Guard ship/helo operations.[5]

CGAS Kodiak had four HH-52s to deploy on board Coast Guard flight deck equipped cutters (e.g., WHEC or WMEC) for ALPATs. Single ship and single helicopter deployments were standard for ALPAT operations. Deployments were planned for 2-month durations and 120 cumulative flight hours for the HH-52s. The

120-flight-hour limit could be raised if major maintenance inspections could be extended or completed at a remote hangar facility (e.g., Naval Air Station Adak, Shemya AFB, and King Salmon AFB). Very seldom did the weather and sea state in the North Pacific or Bering Sea allow for 120 flight hours during an ALPAT deployment.

ALPAT cutters followed a strict ship/helo doctrine based on aircrew survival time. A cutter operating independently with a single helicopter had to be able to reach the helicopter if it went down in the ocean within three hours. Survival time for an air crew in wet suits was dependent on sea water temperature and conditions. In the Bering Sea, the WHECs would keep us on a 50- to 60-nm string if we had good weather and sea state because they would be able to make more than 20 knots enroute and then hopefully find us.

Daniell wanted more information. He knew his helicopter could launch, but what good would it be once on-scene with limited fuel and *Mellon* so far away? Would Rescue-1425 become a liability or, worse yet, another SAR case adding to the worst-case scenario? We understood and had no issue with his logic because no one had confirmation CG-1600 was in any trouble.

I had previously served under then Commander (CDR/05) Daniell when he was CO of the cutter *Yocona* (WMEC 168) out of Astoria, OR, in 1977. He was the best CO I could have wished for with his tremendous underway experience, exceptional ship handling expertise, and outstanding leadership qualities. As **First Lieutenant** (1st LT) and Deck Watch Officer, I learned a vast amount from him. Daniell had served on six Coast Guard vessels and had been CO of four [Patrol Boat *Cape Horn* (95322), *CGC Bittersweet* (WLB-389), *CGC Yocona* (WMEC-168), *CGC Mellon* (WHEC-717)]. Daniell was a stellar officer; he would rise in rank to Vice Admiral (VADM/09) and serve as Commander Coast Guard Pacific Area and Vice Commandant of the Coast Guard.

It was not by luck Wally and I were on this deployment; I requested it as soon as we knew *Mellon* would be assigned an **Av**iation **Det**achment (AVDET) from Commander Coast Guard District 17 in Juneau, AK, earlier that year. Seldom did anyone volunteer for an AVDET, especially in the middle of summer, but we did because *Mellon* was one the best WHECs on the West Coast with an outstanding crew and CO.

1030

CG-1602, another HC-130 from CGAS Kodiak, was flying a drug patrol mission south of the Alaska Peninsula over 600 nm from Attu when they were diverted by NORPACSARCOORD Juneau to the SAR case. It was fortunate CG-1602 had launched early on their enforcement patrol that morning (note- in 1982 Alaska had four time zones which was changed to two in 1983) from Kodiak. Distances in Alaska are hard to comprehend because the size of the state dwarfs any other state and most countries. The route of flight for CG-1602's patrol had cut the distance to Attu almost in half. Wanting more information, *Mellon* radioed the diverted 1602 to find out their estimated time of arrival and any information they may have on CG-1600. I felt very fortunate; I knew the voice that responded from the now designated Rescue-1602, CGAS Kodiak Operations Officer, CDR Jim Wright.

Daniell and Wright spoke directly on the radio from CIC. Queries to Wright were forthright and probing. Wright's initial thoughts were that CG-1600 had missed an approach at Attu because of poor weather, possibly headed south for a short enforcement of laws and treaties (ELT) patrol at low level, and was experiencing communications difficulties, which often occurred in such a remote location. With no emergency beacon or MAYDAY call, Rescue-1602 felt it was premature to think CG-1600 had gone down. Rescue-1602 passed they were working with COMSTA Kodiak, COMSTA PACAREA (Pt. Reyes, CA), and Anchorage Center (FAA) to attempt to raise CG-1600 on all possible working and emergency frequencies.

That made perfect sense to Wally and me. We knew two very experienced pilots were flying CG-1600, LT Mark Whyte and LT George Scherrer. Both pilots worked in CGAS Kodiak Operations Department with us. Whyte was the C-130 Standardization Officer, and Scherrer was the Rescue Coordination Center (RCC) Kodiak senior controller. Both were experienced Alaskan pilots, both designated ACs, and professionally well thought of by everyone at CGAS Kodiak.

Wright, like Daniell, was very concerned *Mellon's* helicopter would be taking undue risk by launching now and recommended a hold on launching until everyone had more information. Meanwhile NORPACSARCOORD Juneau was appropriately pushing forward, assuming CG-1600 had gone down. Juneau requested assistance from the Air Force Alaskan Air Command and the Navy [6]for the SAR case. The Alaska Air Command maintained a KC-135 Stratotanker over the western Aleutians for strategic overseas refueling purpose. The Stratotanker was flying a race track pattern 100 nm from Shemya AFB at altitude (e.g., 30,000 feet). The KC-135 aircraft is a derivative of the Boeing 707 commercial aircraft and had been used operationally by the Strategic Air Command since 1957.[7]

The Navy had a Lockheed P-3 Orion antisubmarine warfare (ASW) patrol aircraft deployed at Adak Naval Air Station 400 nm to the east to Attu.[8] The four-engine turbo prop aircraft based on the Lockheed L-188 Electra (commercial airliner) would launch in an hour to assist.

1035
The Air Force KC-135 was the first aircraft on-scene responding to NORPACSARCOORD Juneau's request. They reported they could not detect any emergency beacon transmission while flying over Attu at altitude at that time. *Mellon* passed that vital information to Rescue-1602 and NORPACSARCOORD, which again made the decision to hold *Mellon's* helicopter logical...nothing to corroborate a mishap yet.

Daniell told Sabo to monitor the situation and let him know immediately if anything changed, otherwise we would reevaluate in one hours' time. The helicopter would remain at the ready for launch as *Mellon* and Rescue-1602 closed the distance to Attu. *Mellon* would remain *Semper Paratus* (Always Ready), to launch, recover, and refuel the helicopter throughout the SAR case.

Wally and I quickly ran the weight and balance numbers for CG-1425 with three personnel on board and a full SAR board. I called Aviation Structural Mechanic Second Class (AM2/E5) Jeff Smith (Smitty), our plane captain and flight mechanic, in the Aerographers Office to fuel CG-1425 with 1,600 pounds of JP-5, which would bring the ALPAT-equipped HH-52 to her maximum gross weight of 8,300 pounds.

The ALPAT HH-52's basic weight was a bit more than the standard HH-52 because they were specially equipped with RCA Primus weather radar and additional cold water survival gear. The radar was mounted on the left front of the helicopter with its antenna protruding from the front of the helicopter. The radar's black dome cover made it look like an off-centered black nose on the helicopter. The radar was invaluable to safely navigate in the Aleutians and coastal areas of Alaska. I only wished we had radar-equipped HH-52s at all our units. It was a lifesaver, especially in low-visibility situations. The only problem with the radar was it restricted the copilot's forward visibility, especially when landing aboard the cutter. The Pilot in Command (PIC) in the right seat had unrestricted forward visibility and performed most of the take-offs and landings when deployed.

Wally and I worked with Sabo and Chief Radarman (RDC/E7) Beckman in CIC on the best routing and waypoints for the flight to Attu. Our intention was to fly the shortest route while staying north of Shemya (Waypoint 1) through Shemya's Restricted airspace, north of Nizki Island (Waypoint 2), north of Alaid Island (Waypoint 3), through Semichi Pass and Agattu Strait to Chirikof Point Attu (Waypoint 4), continuing south along the coast to Alexai Point (Waypoint 5), south into Casco Cove (Waypoint 6), and then south to Murder Point (Waypoint 7).

RDC Beckman and I checked and double-checked the exact latitude and longitude for these waypoints. We conferred with Ensigns (ENS/O1) Missy Wall and Dee Parker, our Helicopter Control Officers (HCOs). They would be handling all communications between Mellon and Rescue-1425 during the mission. Knowing our transit altitude would be less than or around 100 feet above water level (awl), use of ultra-high frequency (UHF) communications on 381.8 would be lost by 20 nm, we would use HF 5696 as the primary comms frequency. The HF radio would work out to several hundred miles however Wally and the HCOs would have to put up with the ever-present static. Static on HF radios was a given especially during daylight hours. I would have had a hard time being a radioman listening to the constant, crackle, pops, and scratchy noise on HF when not transmitting; it was so annoying and would give me a headache after an hour or so.

Wally and I discussed what ifs and any special gear we should take, not knowing if or where the CG-1600 crashed. Knowing the CG-1600 carried parachutes, rafts, survival suits, sleeping bags, and survival sleds, we did not want to carry extraneous gear because that would take away fuel from the weight-limited helicopter. Wally and I were concerned about hypothermia in the cold wet conditions so we asked *Mellon's* 1st LT for ten Mustang suits and wool blankets. In those days, Coast Guard aircrews did not carry hypothermia rewarming bags or heated oxygen on the helicopters. The Mustang suits were well-made anti-exposure suits that provided floatation and weather respite for boat crews. They also made outstanding land survival suits because they weren't restrictive like the water survival suits, which do not allow mobility, especially when trying to walk around. Wool blankets could always be used to maintain body heat even if they were wet. Hypothermia was the main concern no matter where the CG-1600 went down, if it did go down.

With everyone in agreement, except for when to launch, Wally and I left CIC for the flight deck to enter the coordinates into CG1425's LORAN C computer. The only long range navigational system in the HH-52 was LORAN C. We would use it and the radar to cross-check our position throughout the mission. Arriving at the helicopter on the flight deck, I requested external power once Smitty and the rest of the AVDET crew [Aviation Machinist Mate Third Class (AD3/E4) Dave Hissom, Aviation Structural Mechanic Third Class (AM3/E4) Robert Hassinger, and Aviation Electronics Technician Third Class (AT3/E4) Scott Jordan] had finished topping off with fuel. We also requested a regular AC power cord and the "HSK hair dryer" so we could keep the finicky LORAN C computer from having moisture-induced problems.

The cockpit of the HH-52 wasn't always free of moisture and water that seemed to seep in…wearing a wet suit in the cockpit had some benefits when water would, at times, stream in from the upper window/greenhouse area. The LORAN C computer was a new piece of hardware for the HH-52s, and it was not moisture/waterproof. Wally and I had learned from previous deployments to remove the computer every night and take it to our stateroom in a helmet bag, thus eliminating moisture problems. We also discovered that, before missions, a hair dryer blowing on the panel also helped dry it out, especially when the weather was cold and constantly at or near 100% humidity. Armed with aircraft external power and the hair dryer, Wally and I fired up the LORAN C computer. Having the proper waypoints entered into the computer was paramount. They could safely guide us to Attu in limited visibility.

Wally and I talked on intercom (ICS) about how this SAR case was different; if CG-1600 did indeed crash, it would mean rescuing our own shipmates...fellow Coasties and personal friends we served with! We had not experienced this amount of angst in prepping for a SAR case in our short careers. Wally and I needed to compartmentalize; to focus on the case as just like any other case, not dwell on thoughts concerning the well-being of our shipmates, stick to the basics. One thing we knew: during every SAR case "the unknowns" that cropped up would haunt us... figuring them out before launching would be ideal.

The 1st LT and Chief Boatswain Mate appeared on the flight deck carrying the requested ten Mustang suits and wool blankets. It was odd they personally delivered them, but they wanted to make sure we didn't need anything else...they, like everyone on Mellon, wanted to assist in any way possible. We told them the suits and blankets were great, we could not think of anything else. The AVDET crew loaded them in the back of the helicopter. Smitty then asked if we wanted a litter instead of a basket for the case. Wally and I both said "basket" simultaneously. It was the best hoisting device, especially if we needed to recover survivors from rafts or the water in survival suits. Wally went back to entering the waypoints in the computer for our intended route of flight. I double-checked the entries, and then triple-checked them. With the computer routing finished, Wally and I completed the rest of our preflight checks; we were now ready for our second and most important launch of the day.

1045

Wally and I headed back up to CIC for any updates on the SAR case. On arrival in CIC, we could hear the diverted Air Force KC-135 reporting over the radio to Mellon that it was now receiving a strong Emergency Beacon and was attempting to use their direction finding (DF) to get a position. This was the first time *Mellon* or anyone had received confirmation of a crash; the situation had morphed with the sobering fact, a crash most likely had occurred around 0830 local. The KC-135 reported receiving two signals, the strongest signal was emanating from the Krasni Point area approximately 5.5 nm southwest of the LORAN Station and the runway at Casco Cove, with a secondary signal coming from the Holtz Bay area. It was still unknown if the signal was coming from land or water, and the weather still had the island socked in, so the KC-135 stayed at altitude while DF'ing. *Mellon* immediately contacted Rescue-1602 with the information from the KC-135.

On Wednesday 28 July, *Mellon* had been anchored in historic Holtz Bay when Wally and I first flew into the LORAN Station at Attu to meet CG-1600 at the runway to pick up the new helicopter battery. I, like many *Mellon* crew, had read the historical account of the World War II battles at Attu in the book *The Thousand Mile War*.[9] We knew the significance of Holtz Bay and the mountainous terrain that surrounded it. Hopefully, CG-1600 had not somehow flown into Holtz Bay and crashed on that side of the island.

Based on the KC-135 finding an aircraft emergency beacon transmitting from Attu, Sabo called *Mellon's* senior leadership to assemble back in CIC. Sabo explained the new information to everyone, and I provided what I thought would be compelling input directly from the Coast Guard Air Operations Manual.[10] – Aircrews carrying out SAR missions or any other evolving mission in which circumstances dictate a rescue effort of persons or property, shall apply the following guidance:

> *"Saving Human Life- If a mission is likely to save human life, it warrants a maximum effort. When no suitable alternatives exist and the mission has a reasonable chance of success, the risk of damage to or abuse of the aircraft is acceptable, even though such damage or abuse may render the aircraft unrecoverable. Probable loss of the aircrew is not an acceptable risk."*

This was the guiding principal for Coast Guard aviators at the time; the old adage of "You had to go out but didn't have to come back" was not a consideration. Daniell understood but was still concerned because we were currently over 120 nm from Attu, with no break in the weather observed or forecasted. I had been on many significant SAR cases and law enforcement missions with Daniell on *Yocona*, so I understood how he assessed all the information before he made a decision. Daniell wanted to discuss the update with Wright, in Rescue-1602. *Mellon* and Rescue-1602 conversed, the recommendation was still to hold the launch because of the distance, poor weather, and the fact Rescue-1602 was more than an hour out. Rescue-1602 would provide cover and a communications platform for Rescue-1425. Daniell and Wright were both concerned with the last section of 3710 guidance "...***Probable loss of the (rescue) aircrew is not an acceptable risk,***" which under the existing conditions was a real possibility.

ENS Missy Wall, one of *Mellon's* two HCOs at the time, recalls this briefing vividly to this day.

"I thought LTs Peterson and Wallace had presented their case for launching right now extremely well, especially with the emergency beacon now energized and DF'd...we had solid information the plane had crashed in my mind. I knew the skipper would say 'Go,' but he didn't! I was initially shocked, but he was the skipper and what he said was what we did...I learned a lesson that day as the skipper made his decision and Peterson said: 'Yes, sir, we will hold at the ready.' It was tense in CIC; everyone had their say and then everyone did their jobs...no one questioned it. It was a learning experience, which I took with me throughout my Coast Guard career."[11]

Daniell had Sabo and I walk him through the current plan that included both *Mellon's* and Rescue-1425's intended track to Attu. Lastly, we discussed communications. Daniell knew *Mellon* would most likely lose line-of-sight communications with our low-flying helicopter on UHF. HF should work, but sometimes, when in close proximity of the receiving station, HF was not always effective. The intent was to shift communications guard to Rescue-1602 as they were closing on Attu at altitude generating a much greater line of sight for the UHF radio. Based on everything we knew and with *Mellon's* Quartermaster of the Watch reporting to CIC the fog had lifted some, increasing forward visibility now to just over one nm, Daniell said we would launch when *Mellon* was 50 nm from Shemya, 95 nm from Attu, and Rescue-1602 should be inside of 200 nm approaching Attu at altitude. This plan would limit Rescue-1425s risk because we had a divert field at Shemya, overhead cover, and, most importantly, a communications platform in Rescue-1602. As Wally and I moved to leave the packed CIC, everyone told us good luck, Sabo shook our hands, and Daniell looked over, gaining eye contact, and nodded his head to us.

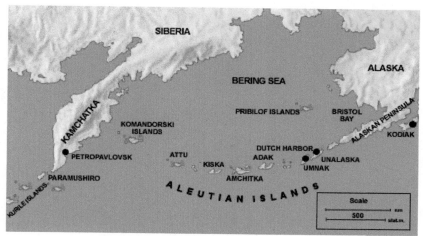

Chart of the Aleutian Chain. U.S Navy.

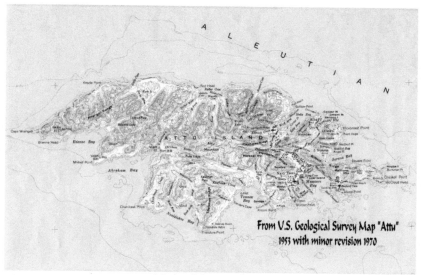

Map of Attu Island

USCGC *Mellon* in Tenmac Bay Attu. Peterson collection.

USCGC *Mellon* on ALPAT circa 2010. USCG photo.

USCGC *Yocona* circa 1977. USCG photo.

CG-1425 Tie Down removal for take-off. Peterson collection.

CG-1425 Airborne from flight deck. Peterson collection.

CG-1425 clearing flight deck to starboard. Peterson collection.

CG-1600. USCG photo.

CGAS Kodiak HC-130 loading supplies for LORAN Station.
USCG photo.

CGAS Kodiak HC-130 offloading supplies for LORAN Station.
USCG photo.

Chapter 2

THE CRASH

"They confronted me in the day of my disaster, but the LORD was my support."

Psalm 18:18

The Coast Guard and especially CGAS Kodiak with its vast operational area covering the entire coastal region of Alaska, the Bering Sea, North Pacific Ocean, and part of the Arctic Ocean, needed an aircraft that was designed to handle long-range patrols, low-level searches, pallets of cargo, short unprepared runways, and some of the worst environmental conditions on earth. The HC-130 was the answer, and the Coast Guard took delivery of their first HC-130 in December 1959. The HC-130 was called the Hercules from Greek mythology and was nicknamed the "Herc.".[12]

By 1982, the Coast Guard had taken delivery of 25 HC-130B/E/H model aircraft. The new four-engine HC-130H model was ideal for Alaska maritime patrol in addition to the logistics missions for the many isolated and remote Coast Guard stations. The HC-130H had the ability to carry up to six standard pallets of cargo and fly 2,745 nm with maximum payload (175,000 pounds). The HC-130H has a wingspan of 132 feet 7 inches, a height of 38 feet 8 inches, length of 99 feet 7 inches' and each of the four the Allison T56-A-15 turbo prop engines develop 4,910 shaft horse power driving the 13-foot 6-inch Hamilton Standard propellers.[13]

CG-1600 was accepted by the Coast Guard in October 1977, and, after modifications for search and rescue, was delivered to CGAS Kodiak for service.[14] CG-1600 had flown over 3,600 hours since new (65 flight hours a month) and only had a short depot-level maintenance period in April 1980 because of a landing mishap that had damaged landing gear doors, wheel well fairings, and skin panels. CG-1600 had been flying without incident or mechanical defects based on current aircraft log book records leading up to the July 1982 resupply mission.[15]

0630

Friday 30 July 1982 was scheduled as the third and final day of the multi-mission Attu logistics and fisheries enforcement deployment. CG-1600s crew assembled at the Shemya flight line for their planned logistics sortie to Attu. CG-1600 planned to fly over to Attu taking the last of the supplies, mail, and personnel, returning to Shemya with Air Force passengers from the previous days fishing group, refuel and then fly a fisheries enforcement flight easterly along the Aleutian chain, returning to CGAS Kodiak that evening. CG-1600 crew consisted of LT Mark Whyte pilot in command from Braintree, Massachusetts; LT George Scherrer copilot from Erie, Pennsylvania; AD2 Ken Sloboda flight engineer from Indianapolis, Indiana; AM3 Dave Weise loadmaster from Lakeside, Montana; AT3 Chris Young radioman from Las Vegas, Nevada; AT3 Craig Michals navigator from Paso Robles, California; AE3 Mark Crocker dropmaster from Vassalboro, Maine; and AT3 Brad Canfield scanner trainee from Oakland, California.

CG-1600 carried only 41,000 pounds of JP4, 500 pounds of cargo, and three passengers. Two of the passengers were LORAN Station Attu personnel, MK3 Ken Stevens from Terre Haute, Indiana, and Seaman (SN) Steve Berryhill from Olivehurst, California. The third passenger was a civilian employee of Chapman College of Orange, California, Ms. Virginia Van den Noort. Chapman College had a federal contract to provide off-duty education programs to remote military installations, and Ms. Van den Noort was working out of Shemya AFB.[16]

0645

Scherrer, CG-1600s copilot, received a weather brief (e.g. forecast) from Elmendorf AFB on Shemya weather (200 feet broken, 700 feet overcast, visibility one and one eight nm, light drizzle and fog, winds 200 degrees true at 27, gusting to 30 knots) and the intended route of flight not only to Attu but back to Kodiak for the low-level fisheries patrol. Weather was not looking good for the logistics flight at that time, but one thing Scherrer knew: the weather would always change.

0715

Scherrer called the watch stander at LORAN Station Attu for his weather observation who passed, "900 feet overcast, three miles visibility, wind 250 degrees magnetic at nine knots, and altimeter setting 29.98.". Actual weather was much better than forecast weather briefed by the meteorologist in Anchorage, which occurred regularly. The Attu weather was above minimums (400 and 3) required for CG-1600 per the Kodiak Operations Manual, so they would give the logistics flight a shot. It should be noted aviation winds are provided in degrees true for forecasts (written form), and winds that are observed and reported over the radio are in degrees magnetic.

This was an experienced flight crew. Whyte had more than 3,200 flight hours and 2,400 in HC-130s, with five previous missions into Attu. Scherrer had more than 5,200 flight hours and 1,800 in HC-130s with eight previous missions to Attu. Sloboda had several thousand hours in HC-130s, first as a dropmaster in 1978 and upgrading to the Flight Engineer (FE) position in 1979. Michals had several hundred flight hours, first as a HC-130 Avionicsman in 1981 and upgrading to Navigator in June of 1982. Young was designated an Avionicsman in the HC-130 in June of 1982. Weise had close to 1,000 hours flying as aircrewman on HC-130s since September 1980 and was designated an HC-130 loadmaster in March 1982. Crocker was designated an HC-130 dropmaster in December 1981; he was assigned as a Scanner instructor for the flight. Canfield had just completed Avionics Technician (AT) "A" School in May 1982 and was undergoing scanner training on the flights.[17]

0740

CG-1600s preflight and start went by the book without any problems. CG-1600 would make the short 35-nm flight over to Attu with a light fuel load to aide in the short field landing at Casco Cove.

0755

On taxi call by CG-1600, Shemya weather was now reported as 400 scattered, measured 1,000 variable broken, 2,000 overcast, visibility 8 nm, wind 210 degrees at 20 knots and altimeter 30.04. All crew members of CG-1600 knew they intended to fly VMC to Attu, land at Casco Cove, offload the cargo and passengers, pick up the returning Air Force personnel on rest and recreation fishing at Attu, fly back to Shemya AFB, refuel and then depart on a fisheries patrol easterly along the Aleutians, recovering at home base CGAS Kodiak that evening. The fisheries patrol was for *Mellon*, as *Mellon* with CG-1425 aboard continued to steam eastbound north of the Aleutian chain, looking for any Foreign Fishing Vessels (FFVs) to board near Buldir and Kiska Islands.

0810

CG-1600 departed Shemya and flew outbound at 1,000 feet awl using the Shemya **Tac**tical **A**ir **N**avigation (TACAN) system for guidance. CG-1600 would fly out the Shemya TACAN 277 radial, which aligned the aircraft to pass just offshore of Chirikof Point and to Alexia Point on Attu. The after takeoff and descent checklist were completed normally. As the flight neared Attu, the ceiling dropped and CG-1600 was forced down to 400 feet awl to remain clear of clouds. The plan was to fly CG-1600 just offshore from Chirikof Point to Alexai Point then turn into Massacre Bay to Casco Cove shoreline and land on runway 200.

Young established radio communications with LORAN Station Attu and confirmed their weather was the same as reported earlier. Sloboda monitored the flight and engine instruments from the flight engineering position. Whyte flew the plane while Scherrer and Michals worked the radar controls to identify the prominent points and shoreline of Attu. The closer they got to Attu the more the weather deteriorated, as visibility dropped. Everything appeared normal to the crew as Scherrer and Michals monitored the radar, keeping them two to three miles offshore of the prominent onshore landmarks.[18]

0825

Approaching what they thought was Chirikof Point, the copilot lowered the flaps to 50% and then at what they thought was Alexia Point lowered the landing gear, completed the before landing check, and passed a report of "landing in 10" (minutes) via radio to the LORAN Station. Passing the misidentified Alexai Point, forward visibility was getting worse, so Whyte descended a bit further trying to gain visibility. Scherrer saw shoals he assumed were at Alexai Point through the lower side of the cockpit window and called for a five degree turn to the right, noting no land visible on the radar for three miles. After two minutes, forward visibility went to zero, and, with Gilbert Ridge not in sight, Scherrer called for an abort with a left turn to fly out of Massacre Bay.[19] As the left turn was started away from the misidentified points of land, terrain was spotted immediately below and in front of CG-1600 by both pilots.

0829

"Pull up!" Scherrer in the right seat exclaimed. "I've got land over here!"

Scherrer added power, and Whyte pulled back on the yoke to climb out...the aircraft immediately pancaked into the southern flank of Weston Mountains near Krasni Point at 138 knots.

CG-1600 impacted at the 450-foot level of the mountain. The main landing gear impacted first, fully compressing, and then the belly of the aircraft plowed in. The initial contact caused the aircraft to rebound back airborne for a short distance and then impact again. The aircraft skidded and rolled up the mountain and to the left, following the upsloping terrain. The aircraft was structurally compromised by the impacts and torsional moments breaking off the empennage (tail) section at frame 737; the left outer wing broke off at wing joint 220, and all four propellers and engines were ripped off the wings by the sudden impact with the ground and rocks.[20]

The vertical G forces on initial impact and forward movement ripped off the main landing gear and ultimately tore the bottom of the fuselage apart; further travel upslope resulted in torsional failure of the remaining fuselage separating the cockpit at frame 245 and the fuselage section just forward of the wings frame 477. Both outer wings were burned from the post-crash JP-4 fuel- and hydraulic oil-fed ground fires.[21]

The aircraft did not just skid 600 feet upslope, it completed at least one rolling evolution as the empennage section had the right horizontal stabilizer torn off and the tip of the vertical stabilizer was badly damaged. The cockpit section also completed at least one rolling evolution; sheared upper antennas were found downslope from the main cockpit during the mishap investigation. The combination of high vertical G forces, impact damage, and ground fires resulted in the nearly total destruction of the airframe, power plants, cargo, and life-support equipment. CG-1600 careened 600 feet upslope from impact point to its final resting point.[22]

Scherrer in the right seat thought he maintained consciousness throughout the mishap, thinking this was it and he would die in an instant as the cockpit section slammed into and up the side of the mountain. The first impact was real loud, like a bang, and then everything was shuttering and vibrating as the cockpit section rolled and hurtled up the side of the mountain. The wind screen shattered, and the nose wheel assembly was thrust up, into the cockpit area. When the cockpit section finally came to rest tilted on its left side at a 70-degree angle, he found himself thinking *My God, I'm alive.* Scherrer's seat broke free from its attaching points and came to rest with him on his back. Unstrapping from his seat harness, Scherrer instinctively grabbed his leather flight jacket off the back of his seat and crawled out the overhead hatch, which was now only about a foot off the ground.[23]

Whyte had blacked out for a short time after impact, and regained consciousness. He was able to unstrap from his harness and climbed out of the same overhead hatch. The left rear of what remained of the cockpit had a small electrical fire burning, and one of the wings containing fuel had broken off and skidded up the slope to rest next to the cockpit. Standing outside the aircraft, Whyte and Scherrer momentarily looked in shock and disbelief at what appeared to be the total destruction of the $7M aircraft. The clouds and precipitation limited their visibility to approximately 75 feet, so they could not see most of the wreckage below them. They immediately snapped out of their daze when they heard Sloboda cry out. He was trapped in the back of cockpit.[24]

Sloboda, Young, and Michals had their seats ripped from their attachment rails on initial impact and were tossed around like rag dolls as the cockpit section careened upslope and rolled before coming to rest. Michals said the noise was deafening as the aircraft was being violently torn apart; it was like being inside of dryer going 100+ mph. Somehow in the melee Sloboda, whose flight engineer seat was behind the pilots but in front of Young and Michals in the aft section of the cockpit, was now behind them. Sloboda was trapped in his seat hanging upside down with a fractured arm, wrist, and back; injured shoulder; and lacerations on his face, with Michals and Young on top of him. All three had survived the initial crash but were far from saved.[25]

Michals at the navigator station had his seat facing the radar screen, 90 degrees to the nose of the aircraft when they impacted. Michals suffered a broken back and severed spinal cord at C7 and T1 as a result of whiplash suffered on impact. Michals was on top of Young, who was in turn resting on top of Sloboda. Young, like Michals, had a serious fractured back and spinal cord injury. Young spoke to Michals, who was beside him, telling him they needed to crawl out of the cockpit because a small fire was burning behind them. Michals was able to unstrap his seat harness and started to crawl toward the escape hatch because he could not feel or use his legs.[26]

Scherrer appeared at the escape hatch and, on seeing Michals, reached through and pulled him outside. Scherrer told Michals to go uphill and upwind from the cockpit and wing area. Young was also able to unstrap and crawl toward the escape hatch; he could not feel or use his legs either. Scherrer still at the escape hatch saw Young, reached through, and pulled him out of the cockpit. Scherrer instructed Young and Michals, again, to head uphill and upwind of the wreckage because he didn't know if the fuel leaking from the wing would explode or catch fire. Scherrer had no idea how badly injured Michals and Young were at that time. With Sloboda still trapped inside the now-burning cockpit, Scherrer reentered the cockpit.[27]

Young was able to muster the strength to crawl and wiggle his way up the extremely steep and wet slope into the strong wind and steady precipitation, but Michals wasn't. Young looked back and saw his friend in trouble, unable to crawl upslope, and told Michals to grab onto his legs and he would pull them both up and away from the wing and cockpit fire. The fuel fumes were very strong, and they both knew fuel fumes and fire meant a possible explosion. Michals was able to momentarily take hold of Young's legs but was not able to maintain a grip. Michals told Young to continue up without him; he would continue to try making his way up on his own. Michals was not able to crawl up the more than 50-degree slope of the mountain as he just slipped and slid in place. Unfortunately, he could only roll sideways or crawl downhill so he tried to roll away from the wing and cockpit area.[28]

Scherrer reentered the cockpit and started pulling on Sloboda, who was hanging upside down, to extract him. Sloboda's legs were pinned in wires and cockpit debris. Sloboda cried out as Scherrer grasped his injured shoulder and broken arm to try and extract him. Scherrer took a closer look at Sloboda's legs and was able to dislodge one but confirmed the other was fully encapsulated in wires and metal parts from the disintegrated cockpit. Scherrer tried to get him free but was unable to break anything loose from his working angle.[29]

The fire was now burning close to Sloboda's head, so Scherrer came back around and stomped out the flames coming from a seat cushion and wire insulation. Needing help, Scherrer called for Whyte to assist. Whyte crawled back into the cockpit and steadied Sloboda's upper body while Scherrer worked to untangle the mess that was gripping his leg. Finally Scherrer was able to free Sloboda's leg, and they pulled him out of the escape hatch just in time. The wing was now fully engulfed in fire next to the cockpit. Exiting the escape hatch, they could feel the heat from the wing fire. Scherrer, Whyte, and Sloboda made their way up slope away from the fire toward Young, who was slowly crawling to safety.[30]

As the extraction of Sloboda was happening, Michals was now caught in the wing fire that broke out beside the cockpit. Unable to hold on to Young, Michals had rolled sideways and downslope when the wing fire erupted around him. But he couldn't roll fast enough before the flames engulfed him. They weren't large flames, but at 2 to 3 feet high for a severely injured and non-ambulatory person, they were huge. Michals fought the flames with his hands to keep them from burning his head and face.

"The fire was so hot it actually felt like cold steel," he remembered, "Cold steel like a knife edge."

With the fire engulfing him, Michals only escape was to continue to roll away. He thought he was going to die, and burning was a shitty way to go, especially after surviving the initial crash! He was finally able to roll out of the flames; however, he sustained second- and third-degree burns over 35% of his body even though he was wearing a Nomex® (fire retardant) flight suit, Nomex® gloves, and leather flight boots. No one saw Michals down slope in the fire area at that time.[31]

Scherrer, Whyte, and Sloboda were ambulatory, so, in spite of the wet and steep slope, they quickly made up the distance Young had crawled. Scherrer and Whyte dragged Young up to a piece of an outer wing panel to use as a makeshift shelter with Sloboda. Whyte assisted Young by covering him with a flight jacket the rain and wind were now their real enemies. With Young and Sloboda out of the fire area and secure at the wing panel, Scherrer asked where Michals was? Young said he was back by the cockpit area because he was badly injured and couldn't crawl upslope.

Scherrer headed back downslope to find Michals. The smoke from the fire made visibility even worse. Scherrer finally saw Michals at the edge of the wing fire below the now fully engulfed cockpit. Slipping and sliding downhill, Scherrer finally reached Michals. Scherrer could tell he was badly burned and needed to be moved; the fire and smoke were still right next to him. Scherrer tried to drag Michals away from the smoke and fire on the uneven ground. Michals cried out in pain from his back injury so Scherrer stopped pulling him immediately. Scherrer recognized the only way to move him was with some type of medical backboard because he didn't want to risk injuring him anymore. Scherrer grabbed a flight jacket lying in the debris and used it to make Michals a little more comfortable in wind and rain. To move Michals on the steep and slippery terrain, Scherrer needed to find a makeshift backboard.

Scherrer was ambulatory, and the post-crash adrenalin rush meant he felt no pain even though he had suffered a broken nose, broken ribs, compression fracture of his back, and facial lacerations during the crash. Whyte similarly was not feeling much pain as he was hobbling around, having suffered a cracked left knee cap, dislocated right big toe, and facial lacerations. Scherrer headed down the mountain toward the majority of the wreckage to find a makeshift backboard. He located the rescue sled near what was left of the SAR bin and took the sled's lid back up to Michals.[32]

Scherrer called Whyte over to assist helping get Michals on to the lid to move him. Whyte's Eagle Scout training kicked in as he and Scherrer dug and slid the lid under Michals to stabilize his back and neck. At one point, Whyte and Scherrer had to stomp out a fire that erupted near them in the soggy tundra.

Once they had Michals on the lid, they slid him a short distance away from the fire and smoke. It was too difficult to move him all the way up the slope to the others, so they left him near a large piece of metal debris out of reach of the fire and smoke emanating from the wing. Sloboda came down and sat with Michals and tried to keep him covered from the elements and the nearby fire that would burn for another four hours.

Whyte and Scherrer called out for any other survivors as they made their way downslope amidst the mass of twisted metal, aircraft parts, and fires. They heard and saw other survivors. Dropmaster and scanner instructor, Crocker, was seated in the right scanners' seat during the approach. Crocker did not strap into his seat, he was trying to take some pictures when landing at Casco Cove. The approach appeared normal, nothing was out of the ordinary, when all of a sudden he saw ground coming up fast in his large scanner window, the aircraft flared, and power was applied to no effect. Impact was almost instantaneous. Crocker was thrown up, out of his seat, and knocked unconscious. He finally came to rest on top of the shelf area above the scanner seat when everything stopped moving. Crocker also suffered significant injuries: left tibia fracture shattering the bone at his boot top and would require a rod to be implanted into his leg; fracture of his right ankle that would require plates and pins to stabilize; compression fractures of the vertebra at T11-12 and L1-

2; fractured right scapula; and multiple lacerations of his left hand and face.[33]

When Crocker regained consciousness, the airframe was completely ripped apart in front of and behind him...fires were burning behind and in front of him. Crocker was able to crawl out of the wreckage and took refuge about 25 feet from the fires. Whyte tried to help move him farther away but unfortunately grabbed Crocker's broken arm. Whyte apologized at causing him excruciating pain and ended up leaving Crocker where he was. Whyte began a search for anything to make Crocker more comfortable. After finding some clothes from a personal bag that had not burned, he bandaged Crocker's head and arm and covered him to try and keep him dry.

The loadmaster, Weise, had not been strapped in his seat on the right front of the seat pallet. Weise had gotten up to complete his safety check for the landing...he had visually checked the cargo and personnel, getting thumbs up from Crocker and Canfield just before impact. On impact, he was tossed around in the fuselage, lost consciousness, and found himself lying outside the aircraft. Weise suffered compound fractures of his left leg, a shattered left ankle, compression fractures of his vertebra L 2-5, facial cuts, and bruising over most of his body. Fire had broken out near Weise and his injuries prevented him from being able to crawl very fast.

Scherrer saw the fire flare up. "Roll, roll away from the fire!" he yelled at Weise.[34] Weise was able to roll away, and Scherrer made it down to drag him farther away. Scherrer brought Weise near Crocker and stomped out another small fire that erupted near them. Whyte looked for more survival gear to make Crocker and Weise more comfortable, not daring to move them any more without a litter or stretcher. Whyte and Scherrer tended to Crocker and Weise by covering them with wool blankets from the rescue bin and a deflated life raft to keep them out of the wind and precipitation that enveloped them.[35]

Stevens had survived the crash seated in the cargo section behind the SAR bin. On initial impact, he was also knocked unconscious by a loose object from the SAR bin. When he regained consciousness, he was still strapped into his airline-type seat, which was folded over backwards. He had no vision in his left eye, it was already swollen shut, and his left arm was badly broken. He had compression fractures in his back at T4-7. Bleeding from the head wound but ambulatory, he was able to unhook his seat belt with his right hand and stand up. Fire was burning all around him. He spotted a hole in the fuselage near him and, with his right arm, pulled himself out the hole. He slid down the side of the aircraft and made his way uphill toward the other survivors.[36]

Ms. Van den Noort was seated in the back far-left seat on the seat pallet in the cargo area. She was strapped in her seat reading *Alaska Magazine* when the CG-1600 impacted the mountain. She briefly lost consciousness, and, when she came to, she found the side of the aircraft had caved in and her seat collapsed backwards with her still strapped in. Fire was burning behind her, and the back of her seat cushion caught fire as she unstrapped. Van den Noort had suffered a broken nose and cracked ribs on her right side, and her left ear was lacerated. At 58, she was the oldest survivor. She made her way out of the cargo area through a large hole in the fuselage where the wings used to be. She was in a state of shock. Scherrer yelled at her to clear the area of the wings because of possible fire and to make her way upwind and uphill to the others. Stevens and Van den Noort were struggling with what had just happened, as they had no aircrew training for anything like this. They were amazed that they had lived through the ordeal.[37]

1040

Scherrer had gone back down to the SAR bin looking for more survival gear when he came across a URT-33 emergency radio beacon transmitter in a survival vest. He energized the URT-33 manually, which activated the emergency beacon with a modulating tone on the military emergency 243.0 MHz frequency.[38] He wanted to make sure an emergency signal was emanating from the crash site because he was not certain if the aircraft's URT-26 Crash Position Indicator was working; it wasn't! Until he activated the URT-33 at 1040 local, no one had any corroboration CG-1600 had crashed. Once he activated the URT-33, aircraft overhead could use their DF equipment to locate the crash site. Scherrer took the emergency radio beacon to Sloboda and asked him keep it with him in a safe spot because it was their hope for a rescue. Scherrer then recovered a sleeping bag and several survival suits to cover the injured.

Whyte and Scherrer assessed the situation: two missing personnel, Aircrew Scanner trainee Canfield and SN Berryhill from LORAN Station Attu; four severely injured personnel; and five ambulatory but injured personnel. They constructed makeshift shelters; the weather was life-threatening because they were in the clouds, with a constant mist and winds lashing them at 20 knots with gusts over 30. Most of the fires burned out, but some still burned in the tundra away from the injured. Everyone and everything was wet. Hypothermia would be an issue if a rescue didn't happen soon.

Scherrer was very concerned about the condition of several of the severely injured survivors and spoke up to Whyte about possibly trying to find help. His assessment was if they did not get help soon several of the survivors could die on the mountain awaiting rescue in these harsh conditions. Both he and Whyte knew staying with the aircraft was the recommended survival technique, but how would anyone find them on the side of this mountain? Scherrer told Whyte he thought the best bet was to make it to the LORAN Station for help. Whyte said his right foot and left leg were not good, so he would stay and tend to injured at the crash site. Scherrer told Stevens and Van den Noort the plan, and they convinced Scherrer they were in good enough shape go with him.[39]

So the three started down the steep ridge to find the beach and head to the LORAN Station. Scherrer was sure they had crashed somewhere on Gilbert Ridge east of the LORAN Station, so once they made it to the beach he would need to turn right and head west. Walking to the beach was more difficult than any of them thought. The ridge was very steep, and they had to crab walk and slide down portions to keep from falling. The wind was mostly at their backs, which meant the rain was not blowing in their faces and eyes, allowing them clear visibility even though they could only see 75 to 100 feet in the clouds. Scherrer kept a small stream that was flowing off the mountain immediately to his right as they made their way down the side of the mountain.

After about 15 minutes of slipping and sliding, they could make out the salt water and a beach area below them. They had to traverse one steep ravine area before reaching the beach. When they reached the beach, they still could not see any familiar landmarks because fog reduced their visibility to one half nm at the water's edge. Scherrer felt sure they were east of the LORAN Station when they crashed, based on their intended route of flight, so they needed to turn to the right and head west along the beach for help. Unfortunately that was not the case, and, when they proceeded to the west, they ran into the cliffs and boulders at Krasni Point less than a half mile from their beach entrance point.

The rocks and cliff stopped their initial transit. Scherrer left Stevens and Van den Noort by the cliffs and kept trying to find a way around. After about 20 to 30 minutes, he gave up on proceeding any further west. He returned to find Stevens and Van den Noort physically and emotionally played out; their adrenalin rush had subsided. In their condition, they were not going to walk back up the mountain, so Scherrer left them on the beach. Before he left, Scherrer gave Stevens his leather flight jacket because Stevens was only dressed in a short-sleeve cotton uniform. Van den Noort was properly outfitted for the conditions, wearing thermal underwear, wool pants, a wool sweater, a Sierra parka, wool hat with flaps, wool socks, and hiking boots. Stevens and Van den Noort huddled together in the taller grass on the beach out of the wind to try and maintain body heat and thwart hypothermia.

Cold and dejected, with the wind and rain stinging his face and eyes, Scherrer retraced his track back up to the crash site. The adrenalin that had surged through his body was now gone; his broken nose, ribs, and facial cuts began to hurt. He followed the same stream up the mountain with blood dripping down his face. When he reached the crash site, he found Whyte, back to the wind, sitting by a wing panel near Sloboda, who had crawled under the panel with Michals to get out of the wind and weather. Whyte was shivering in a survival suit, trying to prevent hypothermia. Scherrer soaked to the skin and exhausted, passed the bad news that he was not able to reach the LORAN Station or get help because of the cliffs, and that he left Stevens and Van den Noort huddled together on the beach, totally played out.[40]

Whyte and Scherrer both knew from their survival school and outdoor training that exposure in these conditions would lead to hypothermia. With the constant winds and precipitation, it would only take a matter of hours. They needed to care for the survivors, because rescue could be a long time coming.

Whyte wriggled out of the survival suit so he could move around and help Scherrer. They improved the makeshift shelters by dragging rafts over to the survivors and covering them. It was exhausting work. The rafts were heavy and difficult to move on the steep slope and in the wind. They knifed the rafts so if they were accidently inflated they wouldn't blow away. They placed the heavy side of the raft with the inflation tank upwind to hold them down. They found survival water with the rafts and were able to give everyone a drink. They talked with the injured crewmembers and told them they needed to stay positive, someone would find and rescue them.

After improving the makeshift shelters, they again assessed their situation. They had nine known survivors, four severely injured and immobile at the crash site, two down on the beach that were not doing well. Canfield and Berryhill were still missing. Scherrer said he needed to go back to the beach with survival gear as Stevens and Van den Noort might not make it because of hypothermia. Whyte agreed but felt Scherrer was getting hypothermic; he no longer had his flight jacket, and his flight suit offered limited protection. Soaked to the skin, Scherrer's body was starting to shake and shiver uncontrollably to stave off the cold. Whyte told Scherrer he would head down the mountain to the beach with a winter flight suit, a survival suit, rain poncho, and some water for Stevens and Van den Noort. Whyte told Scherrer to get into a survival suit to get warm. Scherrer didn't like being immobile in the survival suit so he wrapped himself in a sleeping bag and crawled under the wing panel near Sloboda and Michals hoping the emergency radio beacon would bring assistance.[41]

Whyte and Scherrer knew they may have survived the initial crash, but they were not saved. Their survival clock was running; it was now 1300 local. They had crashed some four hours and 31 minutes ago...as Whyte began to shuffle and slide down the mountain with survival gear for those on the beach.

Overhead view of crash site. USCG photo.

Close up overhead view of crash site. USCG photo.

Close up of tail section facing 180 degrees from impact direction. USCG photo.

Tail Section looking to the west note steep incline. USCG photo.

Above crash site lower debris field looking down slope toward Krasni Point. USCG photo.

Above crash site upper debris field looking down slope toward Krasni Point. USCG photo.

LT Dan Connolly, USCG Investigation Team, next to one of the four destroyed CG-1600 propellers. USCG photo.

CDR Jeff Hartman, USCG Investigation Team, mapping lower debris field slope picture taken to east Murder Point far right background. USCG photo.

Mishap Team Members documenting middle debris field picture facing upslope to northwest. USCG photo.

Chapter 3

INTO THE STORM

"Remember, O LORD, how I have walked before you faithfully and with wholehearted devotion and have done what is good in your eyes..."

Isaiah 38:3

1108

On reaching the flight deck, we briefed the AVDET on our plan and discussed the reported on scene weather at Attu. Wally and I reviewed the SAR equipment onboard Rescue-1425 and asked for recommendations from the AVDET. Wally and I had just flown into LORAN Station Attu on Wednesday 28 July. It had been the first time either of us had flown into Casco Cove and the LORAN Station. The fickle Aleutian chain weather had given us a respite as *Mellon* was anchored in WWII historic Holtz Bay on the northwest side of Attu. *Mellon* had transited 3,493 nm since departing her homeport of Seattle, WA, on 10 July for the ALPAT. Daniell gave the crew a rare afternoon of rest and relaxation (R&R) at the western-most point of land in the United States. Due to our flight on the 28th Wally and I were keenly aware of the harsh terrain and obstacles we may have to face on this rescue mission.

During our cockpit discussion, the Chief cook and a mess cook came up to the flight deck with a huge box full of drinks and prepared food for the helicopter. It was obvious everyone aboard *Mellon* wanted to assist in any way they could. The lunches with extra drinks proved to be most helpful during what turned out to be a long and arduous rescue mission.

Waiting was not a strong suit for us; our minds raced with what ifs and we were about at our limit. Did anyone survive? Did CG-1600 ditch or did it crash on land? What sort of weather were we going to be flying into? Are we prepared? Do we have the requisite skill sets?

Wally and I were no different than most rescue helicopter pilots; always thinking about what challenges we would face to be successful. Famed news reporter Harry Reasoner accurately captured how helicopter pilots are different:

"The thing is helicopters are different from planes. An airplane by its nature wants to fly, and if not interfered with too strongly by unusual events or by a deliberately incompetent pilot, it will fly. A helicopter does not want to fly. It is maintained in the air by a variety of forces and controls working in opposition to each other, and if there is any disturbance in this delicate balance the helicopter stops flying immediately and disastrously. There is no such thing as a gliding helicopter. This is why being a helicopter pilot is so different from being an airplane pilot and why, in general, airplane pilots are open, clear eyed, buoyant extroverts, and helicopter pilots are brooders, introspective anticipators of trouble. They know that if something bad has not happened, it is about to..."[42]

At this time in our careers, we had each flown on over hundred SAR cases, Wally had 1,600 flight hours, and I had just over 1,200 hours in the HH-52. Both of us had flown bad weather, with my first aviation SAR unit being CGAS Port Angeles, WA, on the Straits of Juan de Fuca, and Wally's first SAR unit being CGAS North Bend, OR, on the Pacific Ocean. Both of us were designated aircraft commander in minimum time after successfully completing our upgrade syllabuses at our old units and attaining the 1,000 flight hour minimum (the only higher aircraft qualification was Instructor Pilot, which both earned after ALPAT). Only aircraft commanders could be transferred to Kodiak for the ALPAT mission in Alaska. ALPAT was no place for a new or inexperienced pilot to cut his/her teeth. I had several mountain rescues under my belt in both the Olympic Mountains and the western Cascade Range as did Wally in the rugged mountains of the Oregon Coast Range with its myriad of logging accidents. Wally and I had deployed together before and would fly together when not deployed anytime we could. Wally had seven ALPAT deployments under his belt, so he had seen about every flight condition one could find in the Aleutians and Bering Sea, I had three deployments since my arrival in ALPAT.

Wally first recognized that in ALPAT you were expected to fly in harsh conditions when on his first familiarization flight from CGAS Kodiak he commented he wasn't seeing much of the local area because of the fog, which brought a response from the pilot in command: "Understand, but I can't take us much lower so just move your feet off the rudder pedals and look at the scenery through the chin bubble...welcome to Kodiak!"

Wally and I were very compatible both in and out of the cockpit. I felt Wally was one of the best pilots I'd flown with, not only because he was a good stick, but we looked at flight risks very much the same way: don't take unnecessary risks or put the crew at risk unless it is absolutely necessary. We would routinely request to fly with each other when back at CGAS Kodiak, and, since Wally was the HH-52 schedules officer, his flight submissions were almost always approved.

Wally and I would help the ALPAT shop to get crewmen flight hours by not canceling any training missions because of weather. The single-engine HH-52 was approved for instrument flight but not approved for flight in known icing or moderate to severe turbulence (rough air) conditions. Winter and spring time flight conditions at Kodiak almost always forecast icing and turbulence, which would preclude the HH-52s from flying.

Wally and I circumvented the issue by getting approval for hover flights on a taxiway away from the active runway during these inclement periods. The hover-only flights were OK because if we experienced any icing or turbulence we could land immediately and taxi back to the hangar. The hover flights allowed us to enhance our hover skills and practice most of our emergency procedures. We created hovering skill games that would pay dividends on this rescue. Wally and I would perform emergency throttle takeoffs and landings, which required synchronized application of power, collective pull, tail rotor inputs (rudder), and cyclic to lift off, stabilize, and land. The true test of whether we completed the maneuver in a smooth and non-jerky fashion was to place the straight-necked cockpit flashlight on the flight deck behind the center console and try to keep it upright throughout the evolution. Once we mastered this maneuver and could regularly keep the flashlight upright, we advanced the hover game.

The new game was to disengage the Automatic Stabilization Equipment (ASE) pitch, roll, and yaw channels stabilization; the game required lifting the helicopter into a stabile hover at least five feet off the deck, stabilize for a minute, and land without rolling forward...again the flashlight had to remain upright throughout the complete maneuver to score a point.

When we first started this skill test, neither of us could keep the flashlight upright more than once or twice in 20 or so tries. It was damn hard to keep that flashlight from tipping over because it took very little unwanted movement to cause it to rock around and tip over. After several months of twice weekly "hover-only training flights," we mastered the skill set, and our success rate soared to 17 out of 20. The aircrew also had fun with the hover games. They would watch the flashlight and comment on its tipping movements to rattle us at the controls. Not only did the crew have fun, they were totally engaged as the designated referee. The crewmen had final decision on any disputed flashlight landing event, especially the rolling forward determination. Unknown to me, Wally found a way to ensure the disputes were found in his favor by paying off the aircrew with a six pack of their favorite beverage! Wally, carrying his guilty Catholic complex, finally divulged this to me many years later. The hours spent hovering honed our flight skills, which in the end would be tested throughout this rescue.

Discussions continued with the AVDET on the flight deck about the rescue. Smitty was an experienced SAR aircrewman and plane captain. He knew several of the crew on CG-1600 and voiced his concerns. Smitty was one of the best hoist operators and mechanic in the ALPAT shop. We had flown with him quite a bit and were very happy he was the plane captain for our AVDET. Discussions followed on our need to compartmentalize and maintain our focus on those factors we controlled and carefully assess those we didn't. As a team, some aviators would say Wally, Smitty and I were still "wet behind the ears." However, in our eyes, we had the necessary skill sets and were focused on the mission at hand.

Time flew by, and the next thing I knew word was passed that flight quarters would be set as Shemya was now less than 60 nm away!

1140

Mellon set Flight Quarters Condition 1 to launch Rescue-1425. For a SAR case, the call sign for CG-1425 changed to Rescue-1425, and the Identification Friend or Foe squawk changed from 1200 to 1277. Relative wind over the flight deck was screaming at 45 knots because *Mellon* was heading west on the turbines into the 23-knot head wind. As long as the relative wind was within the 320-040 relative heading quadrant, we were within operational limits, up to 60 knots, to engage the rotors. Anything outside that quadrant and forward of the beam meant a 25-knot engagement restriction. The flight deck was pitching three and rolling six with occasional shuddering because *Mellon* was steaming bow on into the 10- to 14-foot sea state.

Landing and taking off from the small flight deck aboard Coast Guard ships were the most hazardous routine operations for Coast Guard HH-52 helicopter pilots. The Coast Guard created the Shipboard Helicopter Operations Manual (COMDTINST 3710.2 series) to fully standardize procedures for both cutter and helicopter crews. Every operation on the flight deck was carefully choreographed. Taking off and landing aboard ship was not easy; many environmental and physical factors are in play.[43]

First, the landing area was small, 36 feet wide by 63 feet long, less area than an NBA basketball half court (2,268 square feet vs 2,350 square feet). The landing circle (safe zone) was only 24 feet in diameter, the approximate distance of the NBA three point arch (23 feet 9 inches); and the buffer distance (the distance between the ship's superstructure and the turning rotor blades) was only 10 feet at the forward peripheral line and 23 feet when the helicopter was centered in the landing grid.

Second, the landing grid was made of two stacked and joined wooden 2x4s to provide automatic chocking of the helicopter main wheels; it was located in the front half of the 24-foot landing circle. Once the helicopter wheels were in the grid, the helicopter could not roll or slide around on the flight deck. The grid provided a fixed-rotational point for dynamic rollover primarily on takeoff. Dynamic rollover is the rolling motion of the helicopter fuselage around one wheel that is stopped from moving sideways because of the grid and reaches the critical angle of rollover where pilot inputs cannot stop the rollover/crash. I was aware of one such incident that occurred with an HH-52 while taking off from a Coast Guard Cutter in the Gulf of Mexico.

Third, the flight deck personnel had to scramble out of the flight deck nets (suspended below the flight deck) to manually attach the high tie-downs to the front upper sponson, attaching rings above the main wheels, and the low tie-downs to the fuselage, attaching rings above the tail wheel.

Fourth, wind burble off the ship's superstructure caused the helicopter to bounce around depending on the wind speed and direction, and the ship's motion, pitch, roll, heave, and yaw, caused the intended landing spot to move significantly and sometimes wildly under the hovering helicopter. Lastly, the whole situation had limited visual cues because of limited forward sight plane, especially at night!

In 1982 the Coast Guard limits for ship motion were calculated at the bridge on bubble clinometers: pitch limit (the up and down motion of the ship from the horizontal axis) was seven degrees pitch up to seven degrees pitch down or up to a 14-degree arc. At seven degrees pitch, the bow of the cutter was basically being buried into the sea, with green water coming over the bow. The roll limit (the sideward movement of the ship to port and starboard from the vertical axis) was ten degrees to port and ten degrees to starboard or up to a 20-degree arc. At maximum pitch and roll limits, the flight deck was like a carnival ride, the Landing Signal Officer (LSO) and phone talker could barely stand, and the tie-down crew was almost touching the water from their positons in the nets! In calm seas, it is not hard to safely land aboard a flight deck-equipped cutter, but it takes a special skill to land on a flight deck at limits! It was very difficult to safely land on a pitching, rolling, and heaving flight deck. The term most ALPAT pilots used was "landing on a postage stamp in the middle of the Bering Sea." It was not easy.

The technique to safely take off and land aboard a pitching and rolling flight deck is different than any technique taught in flight school because the pilot must NOT fly formation on the ship. All military pilots are taught formation flying, where you hold a constant sight picture, on another aircraft so you turn, climb, and dive as one with the lead in charge of safely maneuvering the formation. The pilot must not allow the sight picture to change throughout the maneuvers until a break-away is given. Hovering and landing on land uses a standard sight picture procedure because the landing spot and reference points are stationary, which requires the pilot to visually maintain those reference points and maneuver the helicopter to the desired spot for hover and landing. An experienced helicopter pilot can land in very tight confines on land without issue when good reference points and the helicopter's power and weight limits are not exceeded.

Landing aboard a ship with a moving flight deck requires the pilot to maintain "a visual relative window sight picture," in which the ship and intended point of landing is allowed to move due to pitch, roll, heave, and yaw. The helicopter should maintain its relative position centered on the flight deck when it is in the level/landing position while the flight deck moves back and forth during the approach. When viewed from the flight deck CCTV, if an approach and landing is done correctly, the helicopter will look as if it is on a string and just walks itself to the landing spot.

A pilot's basic instinct is to try and fly formation on the ship throughout its gyrations, which doesn't work, especially in the Bering Sea. The pilot must resist the urge to follow the pitching and rolling flight deck by maintaining a steady hover that allows the flight deck to move through the referenced relative window. Night landings near limits were extremely difficult. Limited visual cues caused significant issues when trying to gage closure rates and heights above the flight deck. Unfortunately ship/helo pilot qualifications were very limited. It only required ten day and six night landings for initial qualifications and six day and six night annually for currency. Most qualification flights were undertaken in benign conditions to maximize the output and minimize the number of times a flight deck-equipped cutter was needed by each Air Station. I always felt the qualification requirements for ship/helo operations were the bare minimums especially if flown in benign conditions, at twilight or where good night background lighting was available from shore. In the pitch dark of the Bering Sea, at pitch and roll limits, it was a very difficult task to safely land or take-off from a cutter.

In ALPAT this was not an issue because pilots would get a lot of operational takeoffs and landings with a cutter at or near limits. Most new ALPAT pilots would come to Kodiak having never seen a flight deck at or near limits for landings...which really opened their eyes and tested their abilities. Wally and I both had flown missions at the operational limits, we didn't like it, but in ALPAT you mastered the requisite skill set or you didn't fly. Based on our training and ALPAT operations, we were ready for this launch.

The phone talker, LSO, safety observer, and tie-down personnel donned their specialized personal equipment (vests, cranial helmets, goggles, and long-sleeved fire-retardant shirts) and took their positions on the flight deck and in the nets. With no secondary tie-downs installed because of our previous morning flight, Wally, using hand signals to the LSO and the radio to the HCO, requested permission for engine start.

Both HCO and LSO responded with engine start approval. I started the engine using external power, with Smitty as the immediate fire guard; the ship's firefighting team with rescue men were standing by on the lee (starboard /right) side of the ship forward of the exhaust stacks. It was a normal engine start with no problems, so Wally signaled for the external power cord to be de-energized and removed from the front of the helicopter. The high-pitched noise on the flight deck reached a crescendo with three turbines now on line, *Mellon's* and Rescue-1425's. With the external power cord de-energized and removed from the flight deck area, Wally signaled for engagement of the rotors to the LSO.

Every move on the flight deck was deliberate and on demand, based on hand signals from the cockpit to the LSO and then signals from the LSO back to the cockpit and flight deck personnel. The flight deck phone talker passed all requested evolutions to the bridge, which in turn approved or denied all requested actions back to the flight deck. The LSO had no direct contact with the bridge, only via the phone talker, who shouted approvals and instructions to the LSO. The process was standardized and required to keep everyone safe in the aircraft and on the flight deck. The HCO on the bridge and the LSO worked together to provide verbal signals, HCO over radio, and flight deck signals, LSO by hand, to the aircrew and flight deck crew. The LSO gave the cleared to engage rotor signal, after a quick thumbs up from Wally and verbal from Smitty checking the port and starboard rotor areas clear, I engaged the rotors. Wally handled the radio checks and took the numbers from the HCO, I completed the rotor engagement and instrument check, and Smitty completed a hoist check.

1149

Rescue-1425 was pre-takeoff check complete, numbers were rogered, and a takeoff to port (left) with the relative winds at 320 and 45 knots was requested. Take off to port was authorized by *Mellon* HCO; HOTEL flag two blocked,[44] signaling a Green Deck; and the verbal report: "Take signals from the LSO." Wally signaled for primary tie-down removal, and the flight deck crew came out of the nets on the LSO's signal. The flight deck crew worked in unison; they first removed the tail tie-downs (port and starboard) and then the forward high tie-downs. Having one tie-down removed and one on would put both the helicopter and cutter in jeopardy of dynamic rollover if a takeoff were attempted. With all tie-downs off and clear and the flight deck crew in the nets, Wally signaled for takeoff to port. LSO signaled takeoff to port.

1151

Wally and I had never taken off with this much relative wind across the flight deck, so we were a bit apprehensive. I waited for a lull in the pitch and roll...once *Mellon* swung through a large wave, I lifted Rescue-1425 into a hover over the flight deck with a little bobble as the 45-knot relative winds burbled around the superstructure and exhaust stacks directly in front of us. It took almost no power to hover and slide left away from *Mellon's* flight deck and superstructure, as Rescue-1425 was already through translational lift because of the strong relative wind.

Clearing the port side of cutter in cleaner air, I lowered the nose five degrees and pulled collective to 95%, allowing me to transition the helicopter to a climbing and accelerating flight regime. I simultaneously leveled off at 200 feet awl, accelerated to 100 knots (top green line speed for the HH-52 was 88 knots, max red line speed was 109 knots), and turned northwesterly toward waypoint # 1 north of Shemya. Rescue-1425 would have to transit 90 nm of open ocean to reach waypoint #4 off Chirikof Point on Attu Island. The dark seas were accented by the continuous white caps generated by the 25-knot headwind. The gray Bering Sea overcast layer remained solid at around 300 feet, and forward visibility varied from 1 to 2 nm for the initial part of the transit.

Wally worked the radios and radar as we sped toward Attu. He passed an operations normal (OPS normal) report every 15 minutes and added a position report on the half hour and a position and fuel report on the hour. This was standard operating procedure for shipboard helicopter operations because *Mellon* did not have any way to track the single-engine helicopter operating at low altitude.[45] *Mellon* had the same TACAN System (AN/ARN-118) as the helicopter, which allowed us to use the air-to-air mode 63 channels apart (e.g. Aircraft on 23X and Cutter on 86X) to receive a slant range distance between *Mellon* and Rescue-1425. However, the signal was lost at approximately 30 nm because of the helicopter's low altitude. The LORAN C computer appeared to be working fine; the radar picture confirmed distance and range when Shemya Island finally was painted on our scope. Wally was trying to contact Shemya AFB on all frequencies because Rescue-1425 would be flying through a designated Restricted Area adjacent to Shemya north of the island. The flight restriction was a result of the radio frequency (RF) signature coming from the COBRA DANE ground-based, L-band large-phased array radar. COBRA DANE was a very large Air Force system that fulfilled three concurrent missions: intelligence data collection of strategic missile systems; treaty verification; and early warning to the Commander in Chief of the North American Air Defense Command (NORAD), Cheyenne Mountain

Air Force Station, of ballistic missile attack against the continental United States and southern Canada.[46] We understood the COBRA DANE RF energy could fry all electronics, rendering us useless, so it was imperative the system was de-energized for our transit. We definitely wanted to fly the shortest route to Attu and not add an additional 50 nm to our transit by flying around the restricted airspace. Wally could not raise Shemya AFB on working or even on guard frequencies 243.0 UHF and 121.5 VHF. Rescue-1602 heard our radio calls on guard and came up on the Coast Guard working UHF frequency of 381.8 to talk with us. Rescue-1602 was able to contact Shemya AFB and gain clearance through the Restricted Area for us. Having cover and a solid communications platform with us was "worth our weight in gold"!

1240

Having gained excellent communications with Rescue-1602 on UHF, Wally shifted our radio guard and signed off with *Mellon*. *Mellon* would be able to monitor Rescue-1602's transmissions to us, because 1602 remained at altitude, but they could not hear most of the transmissions from us until they arrived in Massacre Bay Attu later that afternoon. It would be over four hours before *Mellon* would retake our radio guard and control. Unknown to us, ENS Dee Parker and her communications team would work overtime to send messages from *Mellon* to Shemya AFB to gain clearances for us to land and operate in and around Shemya.[47]

Wally kept me on track to Attu as the weather worsened as both ceiling and visibility deteriorated. Rescue-1602 was constantly in touch with us, wanting to know how things were going and what the conditions were...it was like "big brother watching out for little brother" because big brother would provide any support they could from above. Once we passed waypoint # 3 (the western end of Alaid Island), we had to descend to 80 feet awl because the ceiling had dropped to 100 feet. Rescue-1602 had closed to 100 nm from us and at the same time started to pick up a faint emergency signal from CG-1600 beacon. Rescue-1602 reported they would proceed directly toward the beacon to provide us with their best estimate of its location. Getting solid latitude and longitude coordinates would greatly help us; we were too low and far to receive the emergency beacon from the crashed Herc.

1300

As we approached waypoint #4 (Chirikof Point, Attu), a curtain of fog enveloped us, and visibility went to less than 100 yards. I slowed Rescue-1425 as we tried to gain a visual reference with the Attu shoreline. Just as we gained visual contact with the shoreline, it was as if we had flown into a beehive, except it wasn't bees but nesting shorebirds by the thousands! The closer we got to the shore for better visual reference the more birds we encountered. The birds were flying at the helicopter from above, below, and in all directions. The old classic Alfred Hitchcock movie "The Birds" had nothing on our situation. This was much worse!

I had the nose light of the helicopter on and slowed to less than 40 knots to allow the birds an opportunity to dodge the helicopter and our rotating rotor blades. This was a technique I had learned and successfully used during some fall SAR cases in Skagit Bay, WA, when the bay was loaded with ducks and geese. A bird strike, or worse ingestion into the open bell mouth of the helicopter's single engine, would disable us and worse yet render us a SAR case. Wally and I discussed trying to stay a little further offshore, because it appeared the bird activity level would drop if we stayed a couple hundred yards off shore. Smitty rogered; he had witnessed enough near misses for a lifetime of flying in a matter of minutes.

We slowly made our way along the southern shoreline toward Alexai Point. At Alexai Point, the ceiling had dropped even further, so we were now down to 50 feet awl with waves of fog overtaking us...forward visibility also dropped to 50 feet at times. Rescue-1602 reported the emergency beacon was coming from a position they plotted as just inland at Krasni Point at 52 49.5 N, 173 08.5 E. Based on that position, we turned due west and headed across Massacre Bay toward Murder Point, electing to cut our transit time and get out of the heavy bird activity along the shoreline. I maintained 40 knots as the weather remained constant...it was bad.

Rescue-1425's Flight Director Indicator from the homing system (DMSE 47-2 RF Homing device) finally came to life. Wally and I could now hear the oscillating emergency beacon on UHF 243.0 MHz and visually see our indicator moving. I was following the indicator on the flight director when we crossed the shoreline at Murder Point. Suddenly a big water tower, buildings, and telephone poles emerged from the fog off the right side of Rescue-1425 at my flight level of 35 feet above ground level (agl). I immediately stopped all forward movement and brought Rescue-1425 into a hover so we could assess the situation.

The old buildings and tanks were from the abandoned LORAN A site, and no one on Rescue-1425 knew what other obstructions were in front of us. Our familiarization flight had not taken us west of Murder Point the previous Wednesday. Smitty and I could see a LORAN Station four-wheel-drive truck, which had replaced the initial track vehicle and search team, parked and running by one of buildings. Wally tried to contact the vehicle on our FM radio as I called for landing check. I wanted to figure out what other hazards we may be flying into, so I landed on an old roadway between two lakes just west of the old station's buildings and some telephone poles. After an uneventful landing in the road bed, Smitty unhooked from his ICS and departed the helicopter to find out what, if anything, the crew in the truck knew...as we had no communication with the truck.

The ground search personnel in the truck at the LORAN A site were taken aback as our helicopter emerged from the fog. The rotor wash from Rescue-1425 was cascading the fog down and away, making a very eerie sight from ground level. Wally radioed the LORAN Station and spoke directly with the LORAN Station CO, LTJG Robert Wilson, to find out what he knew. Wilson passed to us that the truck was part of their search party assigned to the Murder Point area. So far they had not found anything that would pinpoint CG-1600's crash or any survivors. The truck and their track vehicle could only go another quarter mile farther west toward Krasni Point, where the road terminated.

Wally queried if the LORAN Station had any topographical maps of Krasni Point and Weston Mountain area because we felt the emergency beacon was originating from that area? Wally and I were significantly disappointed when the answer came back:

"We have none"! Wally then asked if anyone knew of any manmade obstructions west of where we were. That answer was no better: "No one thought there were any hazards other than terrain further west." Wally and I looked at each other after hearing this, disappointed that we had no more information to go on…a major WWII battle was fought on Attu, and the old LORAN A Station was located out here; somewhere at the LORAN Station they should have had a large topographical map of the area (note maps were found later that day and copied for use by the ground parties). We could see several telephone poles west of us, and we were very concerned about any wires we could encounter. If we hit a wire, which was very possible in reduced visibility, it would ruin our day!

After receiving limited information from the station and understanding that the station's vehicles could not get any closer to the possible crash site, it was up to us. Smitty returned to the helicopter and passed the information that the crew in the truck knew nothing about the crash or what was further west toward Krasni Point. Smitty also passed the information that the sight of the helicopter emerging from the fog had literally scared the crew in the truck!

After a quick internal discussion, we decided to continue to follow the emergency beacon signal up the side of the mountain because we were approximately three miles from the crash position Recue-1602 had provided. We passed on our thoughts and information to Rescue-1602: basically we were on our own; any further flight up the ridge toward the emergency beacon would be a calculated risk. Rescue-1602 had heard all the communications with the LORAN Station, and Wright was very worried we were pushing our limits to find the crash site. Wright brought up the recent loss of CG-1471 in his discussion stating: "Remember CG-1471; don't take unnecessary chances. There may be only a slim chance of survivors if they crashed on the mountain."

CG-1471 was a CGAS Kodiak HH-3F Pelican helicopter flying a rescue mission from Kodiak when it crashed at night on 7 August 1981 killing the crew (LT E. P. Rivas, LT J. G. Spoja, AD1 S. E. Finfrock, and AT3 J. H. Snyder). The helicopter was attempting to rescue a stricken fishing vessel's crew in extremely poor weather off Hinchinbrook Island when the helicopter's tail rotor contacted the water, causing the aircraft to become uncontrollable and crash into the water. Unfortunately, the crew drowned after egressing the inverted aircraft. Wally was stationed at CGAS Kodiak when the mishap occurred and was an office mate of LT Rivas, who was the flight schedules officer for the HH-3Fs. Wright as OPS had made the mishap investigation required reading for all Kodiak pilots so I was familiar with the case and had attended SAR school in 1979 with LT Rivas.

Wally communicated: "Yes, we were pushing it, but we have it under control...We are taking measured risks. We will be hovering very slowly moving like a four-wheel-drive vehicle, as we don't know the terrain or the area."

1317

I lifted Rescue-1425 off from the roadway and began to hover taxi low and slow up the ridge into the fog. We were literally "an airborne all-terrain vehicle" slowly inching our way up the side of the ridge following the distress beacon's signal in a fog that now fully engulfed us.

I was maneuvering Rescue-1425 in a slow and deliberate hover taxi. The winds across the varied topography were not steady or smooth like over the water away from the island, and we were getting knocked around because of the turbulence. Fog shrouded gullies, and ravines appeared in front of us in 30- to 50-foot increments, which was our limited sight line. Not knowing the terrain and having no idea what lay ahead of us made for a very tense situation.

I trimmed the stabilization system on the helicopter to a level hover attitude so if I needed to stop or slow down all I needed to do was release pressure on the cyclic...basically I was flying with only the pressure from my thumb and two fingers (trigger and middle) on the cyclic and with the collective friction collar set firm to preclude any collective bounce in the turbulent conditions. Wally and I had learned that a light touch on the controls was a key to not over-controlling the helicopter; by not over-correcting we also reduced the physical fatigue that eventually would set in.

Slowly we kept Rescue-1425 moving to the west, homing in on the now strong emergency beacon's signal. Wally kept a dialog going with Rescue-1602 as I switched off all communications to fully concentrate on flying Rescue-1425 without distractions. I felt as if we were climbing uphill most of the time; however, in the fog, a pilot can be overcome with false sensations as the only true sense of direction and attitude comes from our cockpit instruments. The barometric altimeter was only showing a little gain in altitude. Flying in these conditions could cause vertigo because the fog was very disorientating; moving in waves through the rotor system, and your visual cues always appeared to be in motion when we weren't moving at all.

Having transited approximately a mile and a half west of Murder Point, we came to a deep and very steep ravine; we could not see across it, and we were being buffeted by the winds spilling through it. I eased off my pressure on the cyclic and steadied Rescue-1425 in a hover. We were getting knocked around in the hover pretty good when I questioned Wally and Smitty.

"Should we continue forward or look for another way?"

"Let's go a little farther," Wally replied. "We're close to the position Rescue-1602 gave us."

"Keep it slow," Smitty agreed, "and I'll continue to call out terrain features to make sure we don't hit anything with the main rotor."

I rogered and resumed a slow hover taxi up the very steep west side of the ravine. I felt better once Rescue-1425 climbed up the west side, and we leveled out on top of it. The moderate turbulence we felt in the ravine had dissipated to only light turbulence. Wally said he thought he saw a glimpse of water and a cliff area to his left as we climbed up the steep ravine, so we were not that far inland.

Crash site photo taken from eastern vantage point near Murder Point facing west. Note deep ravine and telephone poles near Rescue-1425 transit path. USCG photo.

Overhead photo facing runway at Casco Cove, upper right Attu LORAN Station, upper left crash site on mountain west of Casco Cove intended landing site. Note Krasni Point cliff area where Rescue-1425 hoisted MK3 Stevens from the beach. USCG photo.;

Enhanced map of southeastern side of Attu Island.

Chapter 4

Locating Survivors

"What are we going to do with these men?"
they asked. "Everybody living in Jerusalem
knows they have done an outstanding miracle,
and we cannot deny it."

Acts 4:16

1325

Proceeding northwesterly up the mountain, toward the DF, I saw someone to our right front, upslope, wildly waving an orange survival suit with blood dripping down his dazed face onto his soaked flight suit. Wally and I recognized LT Mark Whyte, CG-1600's PIC; someone was alive from the crash!

Wally immediately passed this information to Rescue-1602 and I maneuvered Rescue-1425 for a landing in a flat spot about 40 feet from Whyte. As I was setting 1425 down and lowering the collective, Smitty yelled over the ICS: "UP, UP, UP!" The HH-52's main landing gear was sinking into the soft wet tundra; it couldn't take the load at that spot. I repositioned Rescue-1425 to a different location, which had some visible rocks and slowly set her down; Smitty said it was holding fine so the rotor head was fully unloaded. We immediately had Smitty head up and bring Whyte under the rotors and to the helicopter. Whyte climbed into the helicopter cabin, and Smitty put a head set on him.

The first words out of Whyte's mouth were "Thank God you guys could get here! It was amazing when I heard the helicopter's engine and rotor blades. I couldn't see anything; it was like I was in a dream then you appeared out of the fog. We're so thankful. You won't believe what we survived. No one should have survived that crash."

The first question from us was: "Did you ditch or crash on land?" based on the survival suit in his hand. Whyte said they crashed on land up the ridge. He told us that to reach the crash site from our current location we just needed to follow the small ravine and stream uphill, keeping it to our left. Whyte told us Scherrer had thought they crashed east of Casco Cove, and he and two others who were ambulatory had tried to walk down to the beach and make their way west to the LORAN Station. When they went west they were blocked by cliffs.

Wally explained they had crashed west of Casco Cove and unfortunately had headed in the wrong direction. After that discussion we found out Scherrer had left two personnel, MK3 Stevens from LORAN Station Attu and Ms. Virginia Van den Noort, a civilian, from Chapman College on the beach because they could not continue any farther. Scherrer had hiked back up the mountain to the crash site to tell Whyte they were unsuccessful in reaching the LORAN Station to get assistance. Scherrer had requested Whyte hike back down to the beach with a survival suit, winter flight suit, and rain poncho to keep the personnel on the beach warm. Scherrer remained at the crash site to care for the critically injured because he didn't know when or if they would be rescued.

Based on that information, we decided to deploy a **d**atum **m**arker **b**uoy (DMB) at our current location to ensure we could find it again. A plan was quickly formulated to head down to the beach, recover those survivors, then take the three survivors to the LORAN Station for care and return for the remaining survivors at the crash site. Whyte passed that four of the aircrew were in bad shape and needed immediate medical care. We had no idea how many personnel total were on CG-1600 until Whyte said they had 11 on board and two personnel were missing: one of his aircrew, AT3 Canfield, and SN Berryhill returning to the LORAN Station from leave.

During the dialog, Wally, who had been an Emergency Medical Technician (EMT) before entering the Coast Guard, noticed Whyte was exhibiting signs of hypothermia. He started to shiver uncontrollably, and his speech was a bit slurred. He was only wearing his flight suit, which was covered in mud, soot, and blood and was totally soaked from the windblown fog and rain. Smitty wrapped him in a couple of wool blankets, and Wally cranked up the heater in the back of the helicopter. It appeared Whyte had been caring for the other survivors and had not taken care of himself.

With the DMB working and the DF now tuned to its frequency, we discussed getting down to the water and the cliff area to find the personnel on the beach. We determined Wally in the left seat had the best visual cues to fly because we needed to keep the nose of Rescue-1425 into the stiff and gusting wind. Wally took the controls and picked up into a hover. Wally slowly hover-taxied Rescue-1425 down the slope to the cliff area. We could see that the wind off the mountain was generating "cat's paw" down drafts on the water just offshore from the cliff area.

"We'll take off into the wind parallel with the cliff and then turn out over the water," Wally recommended. "We may go into the fog and clouds for a short duration, but we could let down out over water and regain visual contact with the water."

Everyone agreed with the plan. Wally pulled collective, and Rescue-1425 climbed into the fog and started a slow left turn out over the water. We were now flying solely on instruments. I was calling out a positive rate of climb and altitude from the radar altimeter (radalt). I recommended a heading of 110 degrees. The radar showed us out over the water, as did the radalt, which suddenly jumped to 250 feet because we were now over the water and climbing. Wally maintained airspeed of 55 knots and called for a controlled straight in descent to regain visual contact with the water. He lowered the collective, and we started a controlled descent at less than 200 feet per minute.

At 100 feet awl, I called visual with the water. Wally continued his descent to 80 feet awl, gained visual reference with the water, leveled off, and slowed to 40 knots. Wally continued his left turn to try and gain visual contact with the cliff area or beachline off Krasni Point. As we transited in toward the cliffs, we were hit with the significant downdrafts coming off the cliff. Having entered the "cat's paws" that we had seen earlier, Wally applied power to fly out of the turbulence. We had burned some 700 pounds of fuel already, so we had power to fly through the turbulence. Amazingly the bird problems at Chirikof and Alexai Points were not an issue in this area because only a few birds must have nested in this area and were flying around.

Visibility along the beachline was much better than on the side of mountain as it opened up to 200 feet. We headed east from the cliff area toward Murder Point at 50 feet awl and 40 knots. Wally saw the next survivor, Van den Noort, as she stepped out of the high grass near a beach area waving her arms. She was wearing a blue jacket that caught Wally's eye. Wally wheeled Rescue-1425 back into the wind and headed toward her.

Wally called for a rough area pre-landing check and proceeded to land on the beach approximately 25 yards from Van den Noort. Smitty unhooked from ICS and headed out to assist her to the helicopter. Van den Noort was staggering and stumbling as she tried to walk toward Smitty. Her first words were "Thank God you came! I thought I was hearing things, and then you appeared." She also said Stevens was 100 yards farther west, injured and up by the rocks at the start of the cliffs. Smitty hooked his arm under her shoulder and helped her down the beach to Rescue-1425. With Van den Noort seated by Whyte, strapped in, and covered with a wool blanket, Smitty recommended relocating down the beach nearer the other survivor. The plan was for Smitty to bring Stevens to the helicopter because we could not land in the boulders where he was.

Wally transferred control of the helicopter to me because the right side of the helicopter now had a better view of the beachline for the relocation. I lifted Rescue-1425 into a hover and air-taxied as far up the beach as I could. I landed Rescue-1425 within 100 feet of where we thought Stevens was. Smitty unhooked from the ICS, and headed up the beach into the boulder area in front of us. Smitty found Stevens laying in a fetal position moaning in a clump of beach grass wearing a leather flight jacket.

Stevens said he could not walk and hurt really bad, so Smitty gave us hand signals for Wally to come help. Stevens was a big man, and Smitty wasn't sure how badly he was injured. Initially

Whyte started to unstrap to assist but I told him "No, Wally can go. He's had EMT training."

Wally unstrapped from the copilot's seat and grabbed the first aid kit from the SAR board as he headed up the rocky beach. When he reached Stevens, Wally could tell he was in shock and thought he may have some internal injuries, a possible back injury, and a horrible gash on his forehead. His eye was completely swollen shut, and his arm had a bleeding gash on it. Wally and Smitty bandaged Stevens and figured they could not carry him out, so a hoist would be necessary even though we were near the cliff and downdrafts. Wally told Smitty to head back to Rescue-1425 and relay that we should hoist Stevens and head directly back to the LORAN Station so the survivors could get immediate medical treatment. We could come back and get Wally on the return flight to the crash site.

Smitty left Wally and Stevens to hurry back to Rescue-1425. When Smitty arrived at Rescue-1425, he passed the plan to me, and we readied for a hoist. I stayed on deck while Smitty completed and reported "Rescue checklist complete for a basket hoist."

I completed the pre-takeoff checks and reported "Pre-takeoff checklist complete; here we go."

Rescue-1425 was again airborne, and I circled out away from the cliffs and downdrafts. I only took us to 100 feet awl of altitude because of the low ceiling and circled out a quarter mile offshore from Wally. I stabilized Rescue-1425 in a high hover, noting the main transmission torque at 85% into the wind and trimmed my flight controls. I gave Smitty a standard hoist brief: "The hoist will be a direct delivery of the basket to rocky area next to Wally at the base of the cliff. Hoist altitude will be at 80 feet, giving us approximately 15 feet of clearance from the cliff face."

The hydraulic rescue hoist on the HH-52 was fixed in place above the cabin sliding door on the right side of the helicopter. The hoist had a 600-pounds capacity and 100 feet of usable 3/16-inch-diameter stainless steel cable. Smitty in his gunner's belt steadied himself at the cabin door entrance with the basket hooked to the hoist cable.

I tried to keep Rescue-1425 directly into the wind, but we were getting knocked around as we entered the turbulence area.

Unfortunately, the hoist was going to have to be made in the center of a "cat's paw" at the cliff's edge. The HH-52 T58 gas turbine engine was de-rated 400 shaft horsepower due to main gear box and other rotor component limitations. As a pilot the limiting factor was the transmission in these conditions. I became very concerned I may over-torque the transmission by hoisting in the downdraft area, but we had no other options. In the out of ground effect hover I was registering 96% to 98% torque, with occasional excursions over 100% as the downdrafts hit us.

"We need to expedite the hoist if possible so we won't over-torque," I reported to Smitty. "With rescue checklist complete, go on hot mike and Conn me in; target is at 3 o'clock."

"On hot mike; target in sight," Smitty replied. "Forward and right 150 feet; basket is going down."

With Smitty providing steady and calm conning commands, I crept forward, sometimes looking inside at the torque gauge because the downdrafts were really thumping us. I did not want to over-torque and pop the red flag in the torque indicator... between 96% and 100% Q; I was limited to five minute duration. Anytime the torque registered over 100%, it would advance an elapsed time indicator, which maintained a cumulative total record up to five minutes before popping the red flag. If torque exceeded 116% for five seconds; the red flag would also pop. If the red flag popped the helicopter would require main gearbox inspection as soon as practicable per the flight manual.

We were in a tight spot knowing I would most likely pull 100+% or more during the hoist evolution. To maintain a safe altitude to complete the hoist, I had to risk an over-torque. I couldn't worry about it because I had to maintain my focus outside the cockpit for the hoist. I just prayed we would not pop the red over-torque flag.

Hoisting to a fixed position on land was different from hoisting at sea or landing on ship. It was easier in most circumstances; all I had to do was to maintain fixed reference points in my sight picture, thus ensuring a steady hover for the hoist.

Smitty continued his steady commands as I moved Rescue-1425 forward to the intended hoist position. "Forward and right 100 feet; basket is holding 15 feet off the water." Smitty was confident the hoist would go without incident because this is what we trained for, but the downdrafts were making us dance around.

"Forward and right 50 feet," Smitty said. "Altitude is good; forward and right 30 feet."

At about 30 feet from the intended hoisting position, the right sponson of the amphibious hulled helicopter blocked my view, and I lost sight of Wally and the hoist area below because I had to keep the nose of the helicopter into the wind.

"Lost target continue hoist," I reported.

Because of the wind direction and speed, I could not pedal-turn the nose of Rescue-1425 to maintain a visual reference of the target area. Significantly more power would be required to hover out of the wind and would guarantee a transmission over-torque under these conditions.

Unfazed, because this would happen on many hoisting evolutions, Smitty calmly reported "Roger lost target; forward and right 20. You are moving forward and right; forward and right ten; easy forward and right. Hold. Altitude is good. Basket is ten feet off the deck. Hold. Basket is on deck."

I had several visual references, large rocks and a small ravine, locked in my field of view to maintain a steady hover over the hoist area. It was a tricky hoist as the downdrafts kept buffeting us. Wally would say later that he could see the winds were bad, causing the helo to dance and around making it a difficult and demanding hoist.

Wally had some serious decisions to make, both from an EMT perspective and an aviation flight safety perspective. Recognizing the helicopter was battling difficult turbulence/downdrafts, he knew we had to expedite the hoist, but he also knew moving an individual with possible back injuries quickly was not an ideal situation. He decided the best course of action was to get Stevens in the basket quickly and prayed he did not worsen the man's injuries. After the basket touched the rocks in front of Wally, discharging the static electricity generated in the hover, he spoke to Stevens.

"I'm really sorry this may hurt, but I have no other choice."

Wally man-handled Stevens like a large sack of potatoes and in one motion swept him into the basket and gave Smitty the thumbs up. Stevens moaned but was in the basket quickly and being lifted to the safety of Rescue-1425.

"Survivor in the basket," Smitty reported. "Hold. Standby to take the load; you have the load; basket off the deck, cleared left and back."

I could feel the additional weight of Stevens' 240 pounds as the basket cleared the ground. I raised the collective to maintain my hover altitude, increasing power to the transmission to accommodate the additional weight. I slowly backed Rescue-1425 away from the cliff face and out of the downdraft area.

I regained visual with Wally as we backed away with Stevens dangling below us in the basket.

"Target in sight," I reported. "Cease commands."

Smitty ceased all conning commands and continued his advisory information. "Survivor is coming up; basket is swinging; basket is now steady. Survivor is outside the cabin door; survivor is in the cabin; survivor is out of the basket. Survivor is strapped in; cabin is secure. Ready for forward flight."

I could not believe how quickly Stevens was out of the basket and into the troop seat! He must have had a surge of adrenalin because Smitty said he bolted from the basket and was in the seat in a matter of seconds without assistance.

With the ready for forward flight report, I quickly scanned all my instruments and indicators', noting everything was in the green! I had not popped the red over-torque flag.

I transitioned Rescue-1425 out of the high hover through translational lift to forward flight. We were now headed east toward LORAN Station Attu with three survivors minus my copilot. I now had to handle the communications. I quickly reset my radios and passed to the Rescue-1602 we had completed the hoist, had three survivors onboard, Wally was left on-scene, and we were headed to the LORAN Station to offload survivors. As we continued down the beach toward Murder Point, I contacted the LORAN Station on their VHF-FM frequency telling them the same.

LORAN Station came back with a request to land out at the old LORAN A Station because they wanted to set up a medical aide site closer to the crash site. I explained the weather was still very poor at Murder Point and, since I didn't know all the hazards in the area, I felt it was much safer to bring everyone to the runway at Casco Cove adjacent to the station. I had to drop down to 50 feet awl because of the fog, and visibility was less than quarter nm approaching Murder Point. Passing Murder Point about one half nm inside Casco Cove, it was as if a curtain had been lifted at the start of a new act in a play as the fog lifted.

I commented to everyone on the radio it was unreal. The weather at the LORAN Station was 400 feet overcast, visibility was close to a nautical mile, and the wind was much lighter with no gusts. There was an "Angel Hole" over the LORAN Station. I was able to speed up to 90 knots heading into Casco Cove's runway 020, then I button-hooked Rescue-1425 at midfield and landed into the wind on runway 200. The flightpath to the runway from Murder Point ensured I kept a good distance from the 625-foot LORAN tower just northeast of the runway.

1350

We transferred the first survivors to a deuce and a half truck for transport quarter nm to the station. Whyte and Van den Noort were able to slowly walk with assistance to the truck, and Whyte gave me a thumbs up signal as he was placed in the cab of the truck. Stevens had to be carried to the truck by his station shipmates; he was no longer able to stand or walk on his own. After the truck cleared the area, I immediately took off on runway 200 heading back toward Murder Point to pick up Wally from the beach near Krasni Point.

The Angel Hole remained over Casco Cove, and the curtain of fog persisted as I approached Murder Point. I took Rescue-1425 back down to 50 feet awl and slowed to 40 knots heading westerly down the beachline toward Krasni Point. On the way to the LORAN Station, I had spotted a small spit of land with a nice exposed beach about a half mile down from the cliff area, and I knew Wally would be there waiting for us.

Wally had checked the beachline for any other survivors, calling out as he made his away west from the cliff with the fog and winds getting worse. Wally made his way down the rocky beach and thought to himself he should stop wearing only wet suit booties when he flew off the ship. His leather flight boots would have made it much easier to walk on the rocks.

He made it to a spit of land with a nice beach for landing about half mile from the cliff area, right where I knew he would be. The fog was really rolling in now, so Wally took out the strobe light from his survival vest, energized it, and attached it to the Velcro™ on the front of his helmet. He didn't want us to miss seeing him.

I spotted him right away on the spit with his emergency strobe light blinking on his helmet and passed to Smitty we would land near him on the spit. I went through the rough area pre-landing check list again and safely preformed a no-hover landing on the beach in front of Wally. With a grin on his face, Wally came under the rotors, shook Smitty's hand, jumped into the cabin, and carefully strapped back into the copilot's seat.

"That was not an easy hoist," he said once we hooked up to ICS. "I saw the downdrafts bouncing you guys around."

"Yeah, Smitty kept me out of trouble," I replied, "and we didn't pop the over-torque flag!"

I took off from the beach area with Wally back aboard and headed to the DMB where we had picked up Whyte earlier. Wally and I conversed on ICS that the weather was getting worse with the winds picking up. We used the DF to confirm our heading as we slowly hover-taxied up the ravine west of the cliff area to get to the DMB. It was slow going again, but we only had about three quarters of a nm to transit to the flat spot at the base of the mountain and the small stream that would hopefully lead us up to the crash site.

Wally continued dialog with Rescue-1602 overhead and LORAN Station Attu, telling them our plan. In the cockpit of Rescue-1602, CDR Wright was beside himself. He had been really worried about Rescue-1425 on the side of the mountain in the wind and fog. His thoughts were racing. One of his HC-130s had crashed on Attu, and most of the crew survived; it was just unbelievable. Wright was a veteran Alaska pilot, and he knew the only way to save the downed crew was to have Rescue-1425 take risks. That did not change the fact he felt helpless as he flew a racetrack pattern at altitude over Attu.

We arrived abeam the DMB and were really cloaked in fog and wind. We knew this would be some of the most difficult flying we would face. I briefed Wally and Smitty that everyone had to have their heads on a swivel to call out any obstructions or objects because I intended to hover-taxi in ground effect (10 to 15 feet above the ground) up the side of the mountain to the crash site and hopefully evacuate the severely injured crew.

The process was slow and deliberate. We were fully blanketed in the fog and clouds, with winds of greater than 25 knots and gusts to 35 knots or more. I needed to keep Rescue-1425's nose into the wind to not exceed the sideward flight limit of 25 knots, which could cause a loss of tail rotor control/authority. I canted the nose of the helicopter 30 degrees to the left of the mountain slope and direction of travel directly into the wind. This allowed me in the pilot's seat and Smitty in the crewman's seat on the right side of the helicopter the best visual reference as we inched up the side of the mountain. Wally was forced to look cross cockpit from the left seat and could not see nearly as well.

Maintaining a hover altitude of 10 to 15 feet above the terrain, we moved forward. As the incline of the mountain grew steeper to 40 to 50 degrees, we became very concerned about the main rotor blades striking the side of the mountain or some of CG-1600s debris. It was eerie, almost surreal, as we slowly climbed up the side of the mountain enveloped in the fog.

The first visual crash impact marks, deep trenches in the tundra, appeared like someone had taken a very large backhoe or grader to the side of the mountain. As we continued, ground fire was present in pockets from the CG-1600's 41,000 pounds of JP-4, which had caught fire after the crash. Then one of the two main landing gear and struts appeared half dug into the side of the mountain. Next a bent and broken propeller and part of a T56-15 main engine emerged. We felt we were getting close to where Whyte had told us the survivors were located near a wing panel.

Suddenly the copilot of CG-1600, LT Scherrer, appeared on our right side just outside the rotor arc, wearing his orange flight suit and waving his arms. Scherrer in his rain-soaked orange flight suit stood out in the fog and smoke that engulfed the crash scene.

The slope angle was very steep, at least 45 or 50 degrees in that location, and I knew we couldn't land because it was much steeper than 18-degree landing limit for the HH-52. Wally and Smitty concurred, so we continued upslope about 10 to15 yards and found a small area that had a relatively flat spot for one wheel of Rescue-1425.

Wally and I knew the slope was much too steep for a side or upslope landing, so we discussed just keeping the starboard wheel on the spot with me maintaining position into the wind. Smitty would carefully exit the helicopter on the starboard side, heading downhill because main rotor blade clearance was a huge concern. We estimated we had less than four feet of rotor blade clearance from the side of the mountain in front of the aircraft.

Rescue-1425's main rotor blades cut a 53-foot diameter swath and extended 17 feet in front of the cockpit, with a normal height of 13 feet above ground with the wheels extended on a flat runway surface. With the wheels retracted for a rough area landing, the rotor blades were two feet lower.

I kept Rescue-1425 into the wind, but the wind gusts kept buffeting us and rocking the helicopter. I basically had to fly the helicopter with one wheel touching the mountain. The plan was for Smitty to talk with Scherrer to learn the location of the injured crewmen and if there was any place we could safely land Rescue-1425 to facilitate the extraction of the survivors. Smitty unhooked from ICS and kept very low to the ground by duck-walking at a 45-degree angle downslope away from the helo to confer with Scherrer.

Scherrer was watching as Smitty started to walk away from the helo and thought he would be decapitated because the rotor blades were sweeping so low toward the steep hillside. Smitty duck-walked downslope, keeping low to the terrain to clear the rotor arc. Scherrer realized his observation point was slightly above Rescue-1425, which made it look as if Smitty had walked right through the turning rotors...it was just an optical illusion.[48]

"My God I thought I heard a helicopter," Scherrer said to Smitty, "but figured no way in this weather on the side of this mountain. Thank you!"

Smitty conversed with Scherrer and told him we had already transported Whyte and the other two survivors from the beach to the LORAN Station. Scherrer told Smitty he only had one other crewman ambulatory, Sloboda, and the rest would need litters or stretchers. Scherrer told Smitty it was very steep and sloped everywhere he had been at the crash site but to look around to see if he could see any possible landing site for Rescue-1425.

Smitty quickly looked around while he and Scherrer proceeded to where Sloboda was crawling out from under a piece of a wing.

Scherrer pointed out the locations of the other survivors and told Smitty who was in the worst shape. Unfortunately, Smitty could not see them through the thick fog. He quickly became disoriented in the fog and smoke. Because he was downwind and able to hear the high-pitched whine of Rescue-1425's turbine and main rotor blade beats, he could reorient.

Smitty and Scherrer assisted Sloboda to his feet carefully. It appeared he had a badly broken arm/wrist in addition to cut on his forehead. Smitty noticed how wet and cold both Scherrer and Sloboda were. The mist was now a steady rain in the forceful winds. Heading toward the whine of the Rescue-1425's turbine, they slowly made their way back to the helo. As they got nearer, they caught sight of Rescue-1425's tail rotor, and the main rotor downwash caused larger water droplets to sting their faces. Smitty warned Sloboda and Scherrer they would need to get really low to the ground because the blades were very low and with the wind buffeting Rescue-1425, they would dip even lower at times.[49]

I saw the three of them emerge from the fog and gave them a thumbs up to come under the rotor and to the helicopter. Smitty re-hooked his helmet to ICS and told us he did not think there was any place to land near the survivors and we needed to figure out how to carry them to the helicopter with no litters or stretchers aboard. Smitty estimated two of the survivors were 20 to 30 yards to the right of Rescue-1425 under a wing panel and deflated life raft and the others were 50 yards away.

Wally noticed how poorly Scherrer looked as he came up to the cabin of the helicopter with Sloboda...his nose was broken and face was cut up like he had gone a few rounds with the boxer Rocky Marciano; he was soaking wet just in his flight suit, and had no hat on. Smitty strapped Sloboda into a cabin seat next to the heater outlet and carefully draped a wool blanket without jarring his broken right arm/wrist. Wally told Smitty to give Scherrer a Mustang suit to wear because he was soaked and appeared to be suffering from hypothermia.

Everyone conferred, and Scherrer did not think we would find any suitable material from the crash site to transport the injured survivors to the helicopter. We discussed hovering and hoisting with the rescue basket, but we could not move the injured survivors to a sitting position with their severe back injuries. It was decided the best course of action would be to evacuate Sloboda and return with litters and stretchers from the LORAN Station.

"Hurry back," Scherrer said then exited to the right and headed back to the other survivors with a Mustang suit in his hand.

We discussed how we were going to safely fly back off the mountain. The weather just would not give us a break. We decided it would be best if Wally in the copilot seat on the left side of the helicopter hover taxied Rescue-1425 back down the ridge, keeping the nose of the helicopter into the wind. Wally would have a much better visual reference as we hover-taxied back down to the DMB.

I took over the communications duties and passed on our intentions to Rescue-1602.

"Are you guys pushing it?" CDR Wright in Rescue-1602 asked again.

I could hear the anguish in his voice; there was no mistaking his concern.

"Yes," I told him, "we were pushing it, but we were up to the task and would not take any more risks than absolutely necessary!"

We knew the lives of our fellow Coasties were at stake, and we were the best option to get them off the mountain in a timely manner.

Hover-taxing back down the mountain proved much harder than we had envisioned. Wally had the only view, and he really needed to contort himself in copilot's seat to see where we were going. He held that uncomfortable position the entire way back down the mountain as he deftly maneuvered Rescue-1425 over all the obstacles in our path.

Wally basically retraced our track back down to the DMB with no more than 50 feet visibility as a result of the relentless fog and winds. Once at the DMB, Wally slowly slid Rescue-1425 toward the cliff edge. Again he saw glimpses of water off his left side.

"Just like before, I'll take off into the wind parallel with the cliff and then turn out over the water," he said. "If we go into IMC, I'll turn out over the bay and let down to regain visual conditions."

Everyone agreed with the plan. Wally pulled collective; Rescue-1425 climbed into the fog and went IMC. Wally started a slow left turn out over the water. I was calling out positive altitude changes registering from the radalt and again recommended a heading of 110 degrees. The radar showed us out over the water as did the radalt. Wally maintained airspeed of 55 knots and lowered the collective to set up a slow 200-foot per minute rate of descent to regain visual contact with the water on a heading of 110.

Rescue-1425 descended to back down to 115 feet awl when I called visual with the water. Wally transferred control of Rescue-1425 to me, and I turned back to the west, heading toward Murder Point at 100 feet awl. When we reached Murder Point and entered Casco Cove, the weather parted as before.

"The Angel Hole is still here," I told Wally.

What a relief; it would be an easy flight to the runway again.

Wally had not been with us the time before and could not believe how different the weather was at the LORAN Station. He communicated Rescue-1425's intentions to both Rescue-1602 and the LORAN Station to deliver Sloboda for medical attention, pickup rescue litters and/or stretchers, and return to the crash site. I flew Rescue-1425 on the same track as before down the west side of runway 020 and button hooked to land into the wind facing 200 degrees true down the runway.

1415

When we landed, station personnel assisted getting Sloboda into the truck to take him back to the station for medical treatment. We waited for another truck that was coming with the litters and stretchers. A second truck came racing down the taxiway, stopped, and two crewmen jumped out of the truck. They grabbed two of the litters from the bed of the truck carrying them over their heads toward Rescue-1425.

Smitty ran toward them, yelling for them to put the litters down before they hit the turning main rotor blades! The crewmen realized their mistake and carefully lowered the metal litters and brought them under the turning rotors to the cabin of the helicopter. Smitty stacked the litters on the crew seats and placed the stretchers they brought on the deck of the cabin. The HH-52 had room for up to six litters if configured and stacked, but it wasn't going to work in our current configuration. We discussed how we would be able to fit everyone in the cabin and decided to remove the rescue basket and leave it on the tarmac. We could not use it on the mountain, we had litters we could hoist, and leaving it behind gave us more room. Smitty strapped back into his crew seat at the cabin door so Rescue-1425 was ready for takeoff again.

HH-52 over water basket hoist of a survivor. USCG photo.

"Angle Hole" approaching runway at Casco Cove.
Peterson collection.

Chapter 5

CHALLENGES OF THE RESCUE

"The Lord will rescue his servants; no one who takes refuge in him will be condemned."
Psalm 34:22

1426

I stayed at the controls as we took off and headed back to the crash site. Smitty informed us, on further inspection, the litters were not hoist capable because they had no hoisting cables! We discussed this and, based on the current weather conditions at the crash site, we felt this would not be an issue because hoisting was not a good option with the on-scene conditions.

Fuel was rapidly becoming a limiting factor, with an hour or less left; the indicator was showing 500 pounds, which meant around 300 pounds of usable fuel. Hovering required more fuel than flying straight and level, and we were seeing the high burn rate from the higher power demands of hover flight.

Reaching Murder Point, the Angel Hole disappeared as the curtain of fog dropped down, and I had to slow Rescue -1425 to 40 knots and descended to 50 feet awl to maintain a visual reference. We continued up the beachline directly to the cliff area before heading up to the DMB location. Again, we slowly hover-taxied up the ravine west of the cliff area. It was slow going; the fog and winds would not abate. When we reached the flat area abeam the DMB, Wally passed Rescue-1425's position, fuel state (approximately one hour), and intentions to Rescue-1602 and LORAN Station Attu. Once again, I kept the nose of Rescue-1425 canted into the wind, and we began the slow and deliberate process of hover-taxing up the side of the mountain to the crash site. Having already done this before gave us more confidence we could safely traverse the track again.

Smitty continued his dialog with me, pointing out any obstructions as the impact mark scarring and crash debris came in and out of view. After passing the remains of one of CG-1600's engines, I slowed the hover-taxi even more to a crawl because we knew we were close to where we had picked up Sloboda. Scherrer appeared out of the fog just as before, but this time he was holding, not wearing, the Mustang suit we had given him. Wally commented that was not good. Scherrer was really suffering from hypothermia.

I found the level spot for the starboard wheel and carefully set Rescue-1425 on the spot. With Rescue-1425 back in position near the crash survivors, Wally and Smitty briefed they would take the litters and stretchers and recover the survivors. The last ICS transmission from Wally and Smitty before they removed their helmets was "We'll be quick."

That would be the last communication between us for close to an hour.

Both removed their flight helmets and put on their issue watch caps before grabbing the first aid kit, a couple of Mustang suits, and last blankets from the helicopter's cabin. Wally and Smitty lugged the stacked litters and stretchers out of the cabin and duck-walked them under the rotor blades at the 4 o'clock position. I was able to watch them clear the rotors and head toward Scherrer. They all disappeared from my sight line into the fog and smoke as they proceeded toward the makeshift shelters covering the badly injured survivors.

The winds continued to howl, and the gusts rocked Rescue-1425 several times. At one point Wally thought he could see main rotor blades almost impact the ground. Wally had Scherrer take him to the survivors so they could triage them and as quickly as possible get them in a litter or on a stretcher. Wally's pre-Coast Guard EMT training would be challenged at the crash site.

Scherrer was standing at the wing panel near two survivors when Wally knew he had to force Scherrer to get the Mustang suit on; he was just staring and shaking soaking wet in just his flight suit and nothing covering his head. Wally told him he was suffering from hypothermia and needed to immediately get the Mustang suit on or he would be of no help to anyone. Wally unzipped the suit and helped Scherrer into it, reminding him to keep the hood on because he would lose more heat from an exposed head. Smitty told Wally he thought Michals was in the worst shape. He could not move his legs, and he had bad burns on his hands and head. Wally agreed, and they started to prepare a litter for Michals.

They grabbed a sleeping bag from one of the rescue sleds and worked it under PO Michals so they could lift him into a litter because the sled lid he was on was too wide to fit inside the litter. As carefully as they could, they started to move Michals when a large wind gust hit them, and the steady whine of Rescue-1425 came to life and then it was gone!

Smitty looked at Wally. "Did he crash?"

"No," Wally told him, "Bill must have been blown off the mountain in that wind gust. He will head back off the mountain to the LORAN Station and bring back additional personnel to help retrieve the survivors. He will land at the DMB location and climb up to us." That would be the second time in less than an hour Wally and I would read each other's minds, because that was exactly what I would do.

In the cockpit, I felt the large gust blast Rescue-1425. The gust came from about 20 degrees to the left of the nose, causing a rotation about the starboard main wheel. Dynamic rollover would occur at approximately 18 degrees, and the blades would contact the ground well before that on the 40+ degree incline where I was perched. I had been flying the helicopter just holding the cyclic between my right thumb and two fingers, but when the gust hit I instinctively fully grabbed the cyclic, pushing it hard to port into the wind and pulled collective with my left hand. This was possibly not the best course of action as I may have enhanced dynamic rollover but it is what I did. Rescue-1425 was airborne in an instant and by either luck or divine guidance the rotor blades did no contact the side of mountain. I was climbing and pedal-turning to the left hopefully head back down the side of the mountain. It was not a pretty sight in the cockpit; I was flailing about trying to keep Rescue-1425 from crashing.

I forced myself to concentrate on my instruments and bring the helicopter to a straight and level attitude. I had to lower the collective because I had pulled an armload, which was registering a transmission torque of 100% or more. The flight controls did not have a normal feel to them; I could not trim or keep a steady attitude. Finally, I saw the flashing caution light of "ASE OFF" on the Master Warning and Caution Panel. When grabbing the cyclic with my full right hand I must have hit the ASE disengage button on the cyclic's lower left side. What a mistake! Rescue-1425 was now airborne in solid instrument meteorological conditions, on the side of the mountain which just a short time before had claimed CG-1600, with no flight control stabilization system engaged. It was not a condition I wanted or should be in.

I quickly slid my left hand off the collective and back on the center console abeam the tail wheel locking handle to re-engage ASE. After re-engaging ASE and trimming Rescue-1425 to a wing's level attitude, I felt a calm come over me. It was like time was standing still...many people experience this when in an accident but this was something I had experienced mainly while playing high school and college baseball. I would be so focused and "in the zone" at bat I was able to slow the pitch down in my mind so I was literally seeing the seams on the ball and reading the logo as it hurtled toward the plate...hitting was easy when your mind and body were able to slow down an 80- to 90-mile-an-hour fast ball or 70-mile-an-hour curve.

Now piloting Rescue-1425, which was hurtling down the side of the mountain, I was finally "in the zone" and focused. Time was basically standing still, but my mind was in overdrive as voices were talking me through what I needed to do to survive. Those voices were from all the Instructor Pilots and AC's that shared and imparted their expertise to me from CGAS Port Angeles and Aviation Training Center Mobile. I was blessed to have had so many outstanding Coast Guard pilots (Kinal, Volk, Brown, Luther, Shirk, Dicks, Norton, Wolfe, Crowe, Lish, Johnson, Rohn, McLaughlin, Milligan, McLean, Whiting, and Strong) train and mentor me. It was if they were with me in the cockpit working right beside me...keeping me focused on the task at hand.

I would also say if anyone ever had God as their co-pilot, I did in this circumstance. Calm and confident that everything would be fine, I followed basic pilot procedures with my instrument scan in sync.

First was Aviate: wings level, ball centered, air speed 50 knots, radar altimeter 50 feet agl and climbing, engine instruments all green.

Second was Navigate: heading climbing upslope was 300 degrees so I came left 180 degrees to a heading of 120. I noted time on the clock for distance, and the radar for obstructions. After three minutes, which seemed like an eternity at 50 knots, the radar scope cleared. The radar altimeter now displayed 400 feet agl, the number 1 ADF needle was falling back on the indicator as Rescue-1425 had passed the DMB marking landing spot at the foot of the cliffs. I reduced collective to hopefully regain visual contact with the ground or water. At 100 feet awl, I glimpsed water below as I exited the clouds just past the cliff face.

Third was Communicate: I radioed Rescue-1602 overhead and LORAN Station that I was blown off the side of the mountain at the crash site but I was okay flying alone back to the LORAN Station. Wally and Smitty were at the crash site readying the injured for litter and stretcher transport off the mountain.

Fourth was Plan: I would return to LORAN Station and pick up five fit volunteers to head back to the DMB at the foot of the ravine, land, shut down, and proceed on foot to the crash site to recover the survivors.

Fifth was my personal thank you to the good Lord to have gotten me this far.

Suddenly the reality of what had just happened hit me. Sweat poured off my brow and stung my eyes as my body reacted. I quickly threw those thoughts out of my mind and refocused on the task at hand. The survivors still on the mountain were counting on me to safely continue the rescue mission.

I flew back at 40 knots and 50 feet awl, clear of clouds in the reduced visibility because the fog still engulfed the coast to Murder Point. On reaching Massacre Bay and the Angel Hole, I increased my airspeed to 90 knots heading north toward the runway at Casco Cove. The LORAN Station queried me again if I felt a vehicle, specifically a tracked vehicle, could make it to the crash site? "The terrain is so steep and boggy in areas," I replied. "They'd just become mired down and stuck."

I continued to the runway and button hooked Rescue-1425 at midfield for landing.

1442

I landed back at Casco Cove, and a minute later a deuce and half arrived and stopped on the left side of the aircraft. Being the only person on the aircraft in the pilot's/right seat, I could not make eye contact with the personnel in the truck. I taxied Rescue-1425 away from the truck and turned so I was facing them. I repeatedly motioned for them to come to the aircraft, but nobody moved in the truck. It was not normal for only a pilot to be in the helicopter alone, and I did not want to waste time and critical fuel by shutting down the aircraft. I radioed the LORAN Station to let them know I was alone and the personnel in the truck were not leaving the truck for the helicopter.

Generally the helicopter crewman would come out and guide anyone to the helicopter, strap them in, and give them an emergency exit brief. That was obviously waived in these circumstances. I kept motioning them to come forward and to the helicopter, but all they did was look at each other in the truck. After about 30 seconds of motioning to them to come forward and no one moving, I was really frustrated. We were wasting precious fuel and time.

I radioed the LORAN Station. "I am the only one on the helicopter," I told them in no uncertain terms. "You need to get the crewman into the helicopter ASAP. They need to strap themselves in the troop seats; we had no time for anything else."

After a few minutes, another vehicle appeared, and word was passed as the truck did not have a working radio.

Five personnel jumped out of the truck and came toward Rescue-1425. I motioned the lead person to the pilot's window.

"Get everyone in and strapped into the troop seats," I shouted at him. "We need to go ASAP."

I looked back from my seat to verify everyone was in the cabin and strapping in, then I shouted back at them "Hold on." I pulled power, and Rescue-1425 jumped back into action now with only 380 pounds of fuel indicating.

It had been more than six hours since CG-1600 had crashed as I headed back to the crash site. The Angel Hole was getting a bit ragged; the edges were collapsing in Massacre Bay and I had to fly at 50 feet awl and slow down to 40 knots before reaching Murder Point. I continued at 50 feet along the beach back to the ravine at the west end of the cliff area at Krasni Point. I followed the number 1 needle on the ADF back up the ravine to the flat spot where the DMB was still operating.

I had located the landing spot at the base of the ravine when the fuel low light illuminated on Rescue-1425's master warning and caution panel. The gauge was indicating 280 pounds. Before I conducted rotor and engine shutdown procedures, I contacted Rescue-1602, who still had my radio guard, and passed that I was on deck at the DMB near Krasni Point. And with five crewmen I would be heading up the ravine to the crash site to help bring down the injured survivors.

"Please have *Mellon* as close as possible for refueling," I told them. "I estimate we'll be off line for 30 minutes or so."

Little did I know 30 minutes was very optimistic!

1505

I quickly took off my helmet and flight gloves, leaving them with my knee board in the pilot's seat. I grabbed my flight bag and brought out a gray rag wool watch cap and a pair of heavy-weather leather flight gloves with inserts. I looked at the five crewman who had flown with me and for the first time noticed two were Air Force personnel who must have been at Attu fishing and now were thrust into the rescue mission.

The crewmen were all young and fit but appeared poorly outfitted for the task ahead. They were wearing government-issued leather boots and cotton uniforms. Some had government issued coats, and others wore light-weight rain gear. I was wearing my flight gear consisting of Nomex® long underwear, 3/8-inch wet suit, wool socks, and waterproof Sorel® Pac™ boots. I apologized for having to be so short with them getting into the helicopter, but we are almost out of fuel and time was something we didn't have.

One of the station personnel handed me a handheld VHF FM (COMCO) radio for use at the crash site. I told them to stay close and keep each other in sight because the fog was thick going to and at the crash site; we would follow the little stream off to our left up the side of the mountain to the crash site. I told them my copilot and crewman were at the crash site getting the injured into the litters and stretchers for us to carry down the mountain. Everyone nodded they understood, and followed me as we climbed into the wind and fog up the side of the mountain.

After I had been blown off the mountain, Wally and Smitty continued to ready the survivors for extraction. With Michals finally in the litter, Wally took out a space blanket from his survival vest to add an additional cover and hopefully help maintain his body heat. Wally explained to Michals they needed to leave him and ready the other survivors for their extraction. Wally and Smitty moved on to the next survivor, Young, who was near Michals. Young was conscious but fading in and out. Wally knew his back injuries were at least as severe as Michals', so they had to be careful.

Smitty was still concerned I may have crashed Rescue-1425. Wally urged him on, knowing they needed to ready the survivors no matter what. Somehow they would get them off the mountain. Wally became worried; the strong smell of JP-4, oil, and hydraulic fluid made him cautious about more fires from the burnt wire and smoldering insulation. He stamped out a small JP-4 fire still burning above the wing section in the tundra.

Wally and Smitty readied Young for transport via a litter using another sleeping bag. They carefully placed him in the litter and covered him from the elements. Young said he was thirsty, so Wally started searching for any survival rations.

Moving around the crash site in the fog was not easy. Wally could not make out any large pieces of CG-1600 until he finally saw the tail section. It was resting facing downhill not uphill...which seemed very odd at the time. It was difficult to move around the side of the mountain because it was so steep and slippery. In places, rocks cut into his wet suit booties.

Wally crawled under another piece of a wing and found some survival gear, another sleeping bag, survival suit, parachutes, survival knife, survival water, and amazingly, a pair of size 9 flight boots. Wally tore off his wet suit booties and put on the flight boots, which were his size!

Returning to the survivors, Wally opened some cans of survival water and gave Young a drink, then had Smitty take water to Michals. Smitty and Scherrer took water to Weise and Crocker at the other shelter. Lastly Wally, Smitty, and Scherrer drank. They were getting dehydrated from all their physical exertion. Wally commented he always wondered if the survival water would taste any good...and boy did it taste good! What a blessing.

Wally was very worried Michals and Young would not make it; they were fading in and out of consciousness. Wally knew they need to be kept warm.

"Don't give up," he told them time and time again. "We'll get you out of here and to medical attention. Stay with me."

Everyone and everything was wet with the wind still howling...hypothermia was setting in the survivors were shivering uncontrollably, at times. Crocker was soaking wet under a life raft and writhing in obvious pain. While Wally assessed his medical condition and tried to assure him all would be well, it was obvious he had two badly broken legs and was shivering uncontrollably. Crocker pleaded with Wally to ease his pain and get him warm. Wally "rogered all" and began to stabilize him. Wally became very concerned as Crocker stopped his complaining.

"Thanks I feel much better and warmer now," he told Wally, when Wally had not really done anything yet.

Wally immediately realized hypothermia was now seriously gripping Crocker, and he must act fast. Wally and Smitty searched for anything to keep him off the wet cold ground and rewarm him. They found a sleeping bag and another survival suit by the survival sled. They placed the survival suit underneath him to get him off the cold wet tundra and got the stretcher under him. They wrapped the sleeping bag around him, securing it with a space blanket. They laid the raft back over him and began preparing Weise, who was located nearby under the same raft.

Getting Weise in the stretcher went quickly, but they didn't have any more sleeping bags so they cut up a parachute that had not burned in the fires. Weise was thirsty, so they gave him some more water from the life raft's survival kit. After about 15 minutes, Wally knew he had succeeded in countering Crocker's hypothermia because Crocker asked for some water and was again feeling pain in his legs.

Wally and Smitty were looking around by the tail section, thinking they may need to use it for shelter. It was facing downhill and away from the wind and elements. That's, when they found the body of AT3 Canfield still strapped in his seat, dead. It appeared he had died on impact and did not suffer.

Wally reached down and pulled Canfield's name tag off his flight jacket. About that time Wally heard me calling for them from below. "Wally, Smitty, where are you? We're here to help." I had been gone for just over an hour.

Up the side of the mountain I climbed into the clouds and smoke. It was not easy going up the mountain. We were basically crawling up the steep sections. The rocky terrain and tundra were wet and slippery, until you stepped into a hole of soft watery tundra and sunk to your knee cap. I was worried. We still had limited visibility, seeing no more than 50 to 60 feet; I kept the stream to my left just as when I had when flying. Partway up I had to slow down and stop to let the crewmen catch up. Some of them couldn't keep up, and I was losing sight of the last man in our now strung-out line.

I had hit the stop watch function on my watch when we started up the mountain, at the 15 minute mark I felt better, because we had now reached part of the impact and debris zone area. Next we were walking around a main landing gear and what was left of a propeller. I could smell smoke from the still burning fuel fires upslope.

I yelled out Wally and Smitty. Finally after a few more minutes of climbing, I heard a reply, which brought a resurgence of adrenaline. We knew we were close and had climbed in the right direction.

On arriving at the survival staging site, Wally pulled me aside and gave me a breakdown of the situation. They had found one aircrew deceased, AT3 Brad Canfield, the scanner trainee. SN Berryhill was still missing, and the rest appeared to have serious injuries (mainly back injuries) except Scherrer, who was still ambulatory but hypothermic. Wally handed me Canfield's soiled name tag. Wally passed everyone was very cold, and we needed to work fast because he thought hypothermia was setting in.

The make-shift rescue team worked quickly and tried to reassure the survivors we would get them off the mountain and to medical attention as quickly as possible. We used two men per litter/stretcher to transport the survivors down the mountain to Rescue-1425. Wally thought Michals and Young should come off the mountain first. I recognized CG-1600 navigator, Craig Michals, we were on the Air Station Hangar 4 softball team together. Michals was a good petty officer, newlywed, very athletic, and a good ball player. He played third, and I was the shortstop on the team. Michals had what appeared to be a significant back injury, and his hands and head were burned badly. At first I could not comprehend how he had such significant burns, and then quickly put two and two together. The HC-130 crew did not fly with helmets, and he may have removed his Nomex® flight gloves. The distinct smell from burned flesh and hair haunt me to this day.

I told Michals I would handle getting him off the mountain and to medical attention at Shemya. I told him he needed to continue to fight and stay with me because getting him off the mountain and to medical care would not be easy. I, like Wally, had seen survivors relax and subsequently die before I could get them to medical attention on several previous rescues. As a matter of fact, the first seven rescues I flew as a new SAR pilot at Port Angeles, WA, all ended with no survivors. Several died as we tried to get them to advanced medical care. I wanted to make sure it did not happen this time, so I told each survivor to fight the urge to sleep and not relax as they were readied for the trip down the mountain to Rescue-1425.

1535

I checked my watch; we had been out of communication for 30 minutes already as I could hear Rescue-1602 droning overhead above the din of the wind. I quickly pulled out my survival radio from my vest and tried to raise Rescue-1602 on 243.0 MHz (UHF Guard). The frequency was jammed with the ELT signals from CG-1600. I switched to the other voice channel, 282.8 on the PRC-90. No joy with any aircraft on 282.8, so I shut down my PRC-90. I then tried the COMCO on 21 VHF FM; no joy with any unit...communications was always an issue!

Unknown to me, Rescue-1602 was on the radio discussing with *Mellon* their positioning for refueling Rescue-1425. NORPACSARCOORD Juneau, the SAR coordinator, had directed *Mellon* to standby and refuel Rescue-1425 in Agattu Pass, halfway between Attu and Shemya.

"I'm happy for Juneau," CDR Wright in Rescue-1602 told them, "but between you, me, and Bill, we need to get it right, and Bill requested you to get close to Krasni Point, he is very low on fuel."

Mellon concurred and continued on turbines toward Attu.

Mellon had been monitoring all the communications with us and 1602. They knew I had almost crashed on the side of mountain...but all was going well. Miraculously the majority of CG-1600's crew had survived the crash on the side of Weston Mountain. *Mellon* was also keenly aware I was in dire need of fuel; they had calculated dry tanks about an hour ago.

Daniell decided at the beginning of this ALPAT that *Mellon* would transit to Juneau via the Inside Passage, which meant a lot of attention to detail because some of channels and passages were in very confined waters. Sabo and his Deck Watch officers and Quartermasters had to be on top of their game when navigating, especially at night. Little did anyone know that the Inside Passage transit would be a good workup for the high-speed run *Mellon* was now making through shoal waters off Attu to get in position for refueling Rescue-1425? *Mellon's* crew had also completed several emergency low-visibility approaches with the helo during the early part of the ALPAT to make sure everyone had the procedures down in case it was operationally needed. *Mellon's* outstanding preparations would make the next set of operations go without a hitch.

I took the forward side of Michals litter with a LORAN Station crewman on the rear. We began the slow crawl down the mountain in unison. It was a difficult task to avoid jostling and bumping Michals as we slipped and slid toward Rescue-1425. It took all my strength and stamina to carry the front of the litter down the mountain. My muscles ached and burned as sweat poured off me. I tried to maintain a constant pace down the mountain, but time and time again I would step into boggy area and sink over my knees in the wet muck. I tried to guide us to rockier areas to eliminate that problem, but inevitably I would find a hole and sink again.

1549

We finally reached Rescue-1425 seven hours and 20 minutes since the mishap. We set the litter down outside the helicopter so I could open the cabin door. After opening the door, we lifted Michals into the cabin and slid him inside. I crawled in and around Michals to lift the front of the litter onto the troop seats. Once it was on the troop seats, I secured the litter with seat belts through the rungs of the litter. I wanted to make sure Michals was as comfortable as possible.

"It is good to be out of the rain and wind," he told me, "and I'm glad you didn't have to carry me any further because it was quite a ride down the mountain."

Once I stopped moving, a cold clammy chill hit me. I was soaked with sweat inside the wet suit and like the survivors; I was now feeling the effects of the constant wind and precipitation from the fog that engulfed us. I took off my cold-weather flight gloves. They were useless, the leather and liner water soaked and my hands and fingers shriveled liked prunes. I was very happy I had left my Nomex® and leather flight gloves in Rescue-1425 because they were dry and warm when I pulled them on. I also traded my soaked rag wool watch cap for my flight helmet. The crewman who had assisted me in carrying Michals off the mountain was physically exhausted and feeling the effects of the wind and precipitation too. He was played out, but he knew he could help guide the others, so he headed back up to assist.

I stayed at the helicopter and tended to Michals. I opened the box lunch from *Mellon*. My head was pounding, a clear sign I was dehydrated, and the headache would only get worse because I had not had anything to drink since breakfast. I grabbed a juice box, propped up Michals head, and let him sip some juice. I grabbed another juice box and drank it in a matter of seconds and then another. The cabin of Rescue-1425 was cold, but I dared not start the engine and the heater, which used the same JP-5 as the engine, because we were so low on fuel.

Michals and I talked.

"I don't think I'm gonna make it to the state softball tourney in Fairbanks," he said.

"We'll win it all for you," I told him. "You just get better for next year." In August of 1982, the Air Station Hangar 4 softball team took second in the Alaska state tournament and dedicated the wins to Michals.

Minutes later, Wally and Smitty showed up with Young, who was moaning from being jostled around. It had been a rough ride down the mountain. I asked if they wanted me to go back up, and Wally said no, he would. Smitty and I should stay and get ready to launch. It was not a pretty sight bringing the survivors off the mountain side because the rescuers would slip and slide down the uneven terrain, continuously bumping and jostling those in their care.

1559

When they finally got Weise, Crocker, and Scherrer to Rescue-1425, it was seven hours and 30 minutes since the mishap. Wally, Smitty, and I conferred; and decided Wally would remain on the mountain to lead the ground search. Leaving him behind would provide us the necessary room to transport all the survivors at one time. We decided Scherrer would sit in the copilot's seat and the rest of the survivors would stay on the cabin floor and troop seats in the cabin. Wally with the LORAN Station and Air Force personnel would continue to look for the one missing person from CG-1600, SN Steven Berryhill.

I handed the hand-held VHF-FM radio to Wally in hopes he would have communications with the LORAN Station or *Mellon*. Wally needed to watch carefully for signs of hypothermia with the rescue crew as they continued their search. He had the five personnel get into Mustang suits so they could warm up and not get hypothermic. I had Wally take the remaining box lunches made by *Mellon*. I knew they would need drinks and food to keep up their strength. With the bloodied and banged-up survivors shoehorned into Rescue-1425, Wally and the makeshift rescue crew stood off to the right front of the helicopter while Smitty and I prepared to start the engine and engage the rotors.

I strapped in and quickly went through the before starting checklist, which was called "the wipeout" because HH-52 did not have challenge and reply checklist like most aircraft. Smitty reported the cabin was secure and he was ready for start...When I turned the battery switch to the start position I noticed it was low (<18 volts for a 24-volt system) and would most likely produce a cold hang up. A cold hang up would mean a "motorcycle start" that would require me to modulate the emergency throttle to safely bring the engine up to speed. This was somewhat routine, but we really didn't need a hung or a hot start (>700 degree C), which would further drain the battery and could leave us stranded on the mountain.

I depressed the starter button and clock, engine (Ng) accelerated slowly, and speed selector was advanced to ground idle. Engine light off occurred within 15 seconds but with a cold hang up, so I slid my hand down to the emergency throttle and increased the emergency throttle. Engine temperature (T5) rose to about 650 degrees and engine speed (Ng) rose to 56%. I disengaged the starter, and closed the emergency throttle, Ng held. I switched the battery from batt start to on. We avoided a hot start!

Smitty commented on the light off and asked about the voltage...during the following discussion we concluded that we would most likely not get another battery start from this battery. We obviously had problems somewhere in the DC system that we would need to track down. Rotor engagement and instrument equipment check went without incident...with everything spooled up to 100%, I cranked up the heater to warm the helicopter and cut the chill on the survivors.

1605

I radioed the Rescue-1602, "we found one aircrew deceased at the crash site; have the five remaining known survivors off the mountain. Four have what appear to be serious injuries and only one is ambulatory; one person is missing. Sorry for the delay but it was very challenging to get them off the side of mountain. Wally and the rescue team are headed back up to the crash site to look for the missing person with a COMCO on channel 21."

"I'm in serious need of fuel," I relayed. "My low fuel light has illuminated and I can't risk a direct flight to Shemya."

Just then *Mellon* radioed they were eight nm off the coast in Massacre Bay. They had transited 120.5 nm since launching Rescue-1425 at 1151 through extensive shoal waters, 10+ foot seas, and visibility as low as one half nm, and recorded head winds up to 31 knots. *Mellon* stayed on the turbines, keeping all the rock piles and shoal water to starboard as they proceeded toward Krasni Point from Agattu Strait. *Mellon* would be the refuel platform for Rescue-1425. They were *Semper Paratus*!

1606

Mellon set Flight Condition 1 at 1606 local. I passed my intentions to takeoff and head directly to *Mellon* for refueling. Just before I pulled into a hover, three LORAN Station personnel appeared out of the fog. They had hiked in all the way from Murder Point, which took them just over an hour, and they had followed the sound of the rotors the last 100 yards.

One was a Chief Corpsman, who had brought emergency medical equipment including some morphine. He came to the cabin of Rescue-1425 and Smitty passed to the Chief we were ready to lift off and heading to Shemya for medical care. The Chief said OK and they would stay with Wally.

I gave Wally a thumb's up, which was returned just before I pulled collective for takeoff. I took off into the wind parallel to the cliff and went back into the clouds for a short time as I climbed and turned to the left into Massacre Bay. I regained visual contact with the water at 100 feet awl and leveled off at 60 feet awl. *Mellon* reported they had me on radar, and I should come left 20 degrees. I adjusted Rescue-1425's heading and was now painting *Mellon* on my radar.

I completed my pre-landing check and briefed LT Scherrer on the upcoming shipboard landing. Knowing Scherrer had just been through a horrific crash, I did not want him to touch or block the flight controls (dual cyclic and collective for control from either pilot's seat) because they would be easy to grab or block during a shipboard landing. I quickly instructed Scherrer over ICS we needed to land on *Mellon* for fuel.

"Please keep your hands and feet away from the flight controls," I told him. "To you, landing aboard ship may look like we're going to crash. The clearances are tight, and if you have never observed or flown a shipboard landing, it may be very alarming. Please know we aren't going to crash. I've got this. If you need to, just close your eyes."

Scherrer rogered all. He had flown in helicopters before but had never seen or been a part of a shipboard landing. *Mellon* was again briefed we were flying with the low fuel light so needed to land ASAP. We would take on 600 pounds of fuel and then immediately launch for Shemya because all the seriously injured personnel were aboard the aircraft. The decision was made to refuel the helicopter with all personnel remaining on board; it was determined getting the survivors to advanced medical care (equipment and personnel) outweighed the risk of refueling with everyone onboard. The HH-52 had no pressure fueling capability and no way to hot refuel. We could only gravity refuel using a standard fuel nozzle (e.g. gas station type).

1611

The numbers were past to Rescue-1425, and I rogered with a landing check complete. I requested the Executive Officer (XO) come to the flight deck after shutdown so I could pass him the name tag of the deceased aircrewman. I knew a female seaman aboard *Mellon* had a brother on CG-1600 and felt it would be a horrible way to find out her brother died via a radio call or shipboard chatter. What were the odds that siblings, both in the Coast Guard, would be involved in a tragic crash and heroic rescue in the remotest of locations at Attu Island, AK? Fortunately for SN Debbie Young, sister of AT3 Young, her brother was alive but critically injured aboard Rescue-1425.

Sea conditions were basically calm as a result of the lee formed by Attu. *Mellon* had a limited pitch of two degrees and roll of four degrees, with reduced visibility of one quarter mile, ceiling of 200 feet and winds gusting to 30 knots. I finally could make out *Mellon's* stern and flight deck at about 100 yards. The HCO passed green deck and to take signals from the LSO for landing and refuel operations. I brought Rescue-1425 into a stable high hover two rotor diameters off the stern and proceeded to hover-taxi in for landing.

The signals from the LSO were short and sweet, forward signal twice and then the land signal. I glanced over at Scherrer and saw him squirming in the copilot seat as we crossed the fantail and came over the flight deck for the landing, but he did not touch or block the flight controls. Smitty called the tailwheel over the flight deck as I slid forward over the landing circle, hovered momentarily, and landed in the center of the grid.

1613
I immediately signaled for primary tie-downs and, when the install was completed, requested engine and rotor shutdown; I completed those shutdown procedures immediately. Scherrer looked over at me; his eyes were like saucers.

"You just scared the hell out of me. I can't believe you land on a cutter like that all the time? I don't ever want to do that again!"

"That is what we do for a living," I said with a laugh, "and get paid the big bucks for it!"

"No thanks!" Scherrer said, knowing ALPAT pilots didn't get paid any more than any other Coast Guard pilot.

"Just relax and we'll get you to Shemya," I told him. Then I signaled for the refueling operations and the flight deck was bursting with activity.

The tie-down crew on the starboard side of *Mellon* could see the survivors lying in the cabin of Rescue-1425. What they saw and smelled would stay with them for the rest of their careers. The litters and stretchers with the survivors were covered in mud, blood, and soot. Smoke from the crash site permeated the survivors' clothing and rescue gear. Looking like he had been to war, his red wet suit stained in blood and mud, Smitty handled the refueling operations with *Mellon's* crew.

I signaled for the XO, who was now on the flight deck to come to the helo so I could pass the name tag of the deceased aircrewman, AT3 Canfield. I passed the name tag to him so he could send the name of the deceased in the **situation report** (SITREP). The XO had something for me; he handed me a can of Dr. Pepper to drink. CAPT Daniell knew that was my soda of choice from our time on *Yocona*. I was grateful for the soda. I was very thirsty and still dehydrated with all the flying and physical exertion up and down the mountain.

Refueling to 600 pounds was completed quickly, and the rest of my AVDET (Hassinger, Hissom and Jordan) stepped up as they found ways to speed up the process. I signaled for external power, engine start, and rotor engagement...which were immediately approved. Hissom hooked up external power because we knew the battery would not start the engine. Smitty and I quickly completed the engine start, Hissom removed the external power cable, and I initiated rotor engagement with approval from the LSO. No instrument check was required so, with all gauges in the green, I immediately requested permission to take off to port. HCO affirmed takeoff to port, the numbers remained the same. LSO signaled primary tie-down removal at my request, and I signaled for takeoff. LSO responded with takeoff to port.

1622

I confirmed with Smitty that all was good in the cabin on intercom, and looked over at Scherrer, who nodded his head affirmative. We were ready for takeoff, and I pulled collective. Rescue-1425 was airborne as we hovered over the flight deck. I slid the helo to port, clear of all obstructions, then rocked the nose forward to an accelerating attitude and increased power to the rotor system enroute Shemya AFB. It was truly amazing. Because the flight deck crew and AVDET worked as one, **it took only nine, repeat nine minutes for Rescue-1425 to land, shut down, refuel, restart, and takeoff again from** *Mellon*. It would normally take at least 30 minutes to accomplish this tasking. The remarkable teamwork of the AVDET and *Mellon* personnel allowed them to perform flawlessly under extremely stressful conditions. The AVDET had never observed a finer flight deck or CIC crew on ALPAT. In 26 years of operational flying and three years as a ship-helo/HH-52/HH-65 standardization instructor operating from the Coast Guard Aviation Training Center in Mobile, AL, I never witnessed another flight deck and CIC crew that operated as efficiently as those on *Mellon* that day.

CGAS Kodiak had launched CG-1500 from Kodiak, piloted by LCDR Steve Vagts and LT Bill Paradise, with an additional aircrew including pilots LCDR Kyle Jones (CGAS Kodiak Flight Safety Officer) and LT Dave Hoover. The aircraft was also staffed with medical personnel and equipment led by CAPT Marty Nemiroff, Chief Flight Surgeon at Kodiak. Dr. Nemiroff cherry-picked several medical corpsmen along with emergency medical supplies and equipment to assist in caring for survivors of the crash.[50]

CG-1500's arrival at Shemya AFB would coincide with my takeoff from *Mellon*. CG-1500 shot an instrument approach and broke out at 400 feet from the fog layer and safely landed. Immediately on arrival, Dr. Nemiroff and his team conferred with Shemya AFB medical personnel to set up the Triage Center at the operations terminal. Shemya AFB personnel worked tirelessly alongside Coast Guard personnel to assist in any way possible. Rescue-1602 followed them, shooting the instrument approach, also breaking out around 400 feet, and safely landing at Shemya before my arrival.

The weather stayed poor as I flew Rescue-1425 at 70 feet awl and 80 knots across Massacre Bay, Agattu Strait, south of Alaid and Nizki Islands, and across the 35 nm to Shemya, with visibility between one half to one nm. I was able to climb 150 feet awl because the ceiling raised approaching Shemya from the west. Scherrer assisted me in opening up the flight supplement for Shemya AFB because I had never landed there. Scherrer was showing me the runway configuration from the flight supplement page when the weather opened up.

"I think 10,000 feet of runway would be sufficient for you to land," he commented sarcastically over the intercom, "based on our recent landing on the cutter's postage stamp size flight deck."

I was amazed at the dialog and chuckled at the comment. I agreed, but I wanted to know where I needed to land to get the survivors to triage.

As I was nearing final approach at the west end of runway 10, I heard an Air Force KC-135 medevac aircraft shooting an approach from the east to runway 28 on Shemya's frequency. At three quarters of an nm off the end of the runway at 150 feet awl and less than one mile visibility, I requested the medevac aircraft on approach wave off because we really didn't need any conflict approaching from the opposite direction. The Air Force pilot announced his wave off without issue.

1648

I landed Rescue-1425 and slowly started ground-taxing at eight hours and 19 minutes since the mishap and just over 45 minutes since we left the side of the mountain! Shemya ground control passed the operations terminal was set up as the Triage Center and for me to proceed to that location. I taxied toward the Operations Terminal, Scherrer pointed out, when it came into view. Near the terminal, an Air Force line crewman jogged out wearing his line crew safety gear (goggles, cranial helmet, ear plugs, yellow vest, and wands). He provided taxi directions to a spot within 75 feet of the Triage Center with my nose into the wind. I set the parking brake and completed engine and rotor shutdown.

When the rotors stopped, emergency medical personnel ran to the helicopter and started to tend to the survivors. It was a huge relief to get our fellow Coasties to advanced medical care! I breathed a sigh of relief, and then assisted Scherrer out of his seat harness and off the helicopter. A corpsman took Scherrer by the arm and led him into the terminal turned Triage Center. Scherrer looked back toward me and Rescue-1425 mouthing "Thank you" as he made his way inside.

Smitty helped carry in one of the litters and then headed back out to Rescue-1425 to refuel and prepare to fly back to LORAN Station Attu for the other four survivors. As Smitty and I finished refueling to 1000 pounds, LCDR Vagts, who had just flown in on CG-1500, brought out two box lunches and drinks for us. We quickly dug into the box lunches. Our last meal had been breakfast on *Mellon* at 0700, which seemed ages ago.

Smitty and I were then summoned inside the operations terminal to a back room where Wright along with Hoover were conferring with RCC Kodiak and NORPACSARCOORD Juneau. Wright could tell Smitty and I were very fatigued. Our faces and wet suits told the story; we were covered in mud, soot, and some blood. Wright was concerned about me flying single piloted again because the weather was not getting any better. We had already flown for over five hours that day and had gone up and down the mountain recovering the survivors. Wright felt having a fresh set of eyes on board would help. He suggested LCDR Kyle Jones, CGAS Kodiak Safety officer, who had flown helicopters earlier in his career, fly with me as the copilot/safety pilot. Smitty and I had no problem with Jones flying with us; another set of fresh eyes was always good, especially in the conditions we were flying in.

I asked if they could launch a Herc for communications because I knew we would not be able to communicate with *Mellon* or the LORAN Station if I had to stay as low as I did coming to Shemya. At first someone said no, but in the end LCDR Vagts said yes, he would launch and provide communications cover for us.

Meanwhile the emergency medical teams were busy tending to the survivors. The operations terminal was now a field hospital with a flight surgeon and medical personnel trying to stabilize the survivors before they were further transported to Anchorage area hospitals. The Air Force KC-135 medevac aircraft from Eielson AFB, outside of Fairbanks, AK, landed and taxied in after their second approach.

Meanwhile on Weston Mountain, after watching Rescue-1425 take off into the fog with the survivors, Wally led the team of volunteers back up to the crash site. Before he started up the mountain, he made sure every Mustang suit they had was donned. The Mustang suits proved to be a God send and none of the rescuers had to be rescued from the elements.

Wally was worried that someone on the team would get lost, so he carefully explained that each man had to be responsible for a partner. He made sure they understood the significance of the crash and crash site integrity, which meant they should not move or remove any of the aircraft parts or crash debris. Wally led the combined Coast Guard and Air Force team up to the crash site so they could call out for and search for SN Berryhill.

All the LORAN Station crew knew Berryhill very well and were anxious to find him. Wally had taken his small 35-mm camera from his flight bag, so he was able to take the first pictures of the crash site shrouded in fog and rain. Wally and his team scoured the main crash site debris line initially, then fanned out first to the west of the debris field and then east of the debris field to see if they could find Berryhill or any signs someone had walked away from the crash. When one of the team would call out for Berryhill, they would all pause and listen for a reply. The only thing they heard was the incessant wind.

After several hours of searching, Wally had the team gathered, out of the weather, in the tail section of CG-1600 for a break. He broke out the box lunches *Mellon* had prepared, and they ate and drank everything.

Wally noticed the tail section was on a very steep section of the ridge, and, when the wind buffeted, it felt like they could possible slide down the mountain like a big toboggan (Author's note: 2 years after the mishap, the tail section slid approximately 100 yards down the mountain as a result of heavy winds).

It was rough going on the side of the mountain, and most of the team was physically and emotionally played out after climbing up and down several times. Wally had made sure the team did not disturb any of the crash debris so the investigation teams could do their job.

Even though it would be daylight for several more hours, visibility was waning in the unrelenting fog and wind. Not wanting anyone to get injured or to spend the night on the mountain, he planned one last sweep of the crash site from top to bottom. They would then make the hour plus walk out to Murder Point.

Wally had limited direct communication with *Mellon* and only indirect communication with the LORAN Station; the hand-held VHF FM radio did not have a line of sight to the receiver in Casco Cove. *Mellon* would relay their progress and plan to the LORAN Station.

The final sweep of the crash site found no sign of SN Berryhill. As Wally and search party proceeded down the mountain to the DMB, Wally quickly realized the adrenaline and "can do spirit" were waning fast. His legs were rubbery, and the exertion needed to overcome the constriction of the tight wet suit made it more difficult to walk. With Wally's ever present "the glass is half full optimism," he thought to himself if he collapsed or fell the younger stronger Coasties and Air Force personnel in front of him would break his fall and be able to drag him off the mountain to the awaiting truck.

Everyone on the team slid and fell several times before they finally reached the flat area by the DMB. Wally was still concerned they could get lost with the limited visibility, so he led the team toward the beach. Keeping the beach area visible on his right, he proceeded west above the beach to Murder Point. It was basically a forced march that took every ounce of energy they had. They kept each other in sight and took several breaks.

Near Murder Point, the hand-held radio came to life, and Wally was able to communicate directly with the LORAN Station. The station personnel had become worried when the search team had started off the mountain around 1600 and had not reached Murder Point in over an hour. To ensure they were heading directly to the vehicles, the drivers started to honk the horns to guide the search team.

Finally reaching Murder Point, the team covered in mud and soot, extremely cold from the wind and fog, they all plied into the warm and dry trucks to return to Casco Cove. Everyone was disappointed they had not found SN Berryhill.

Wally and the team collapsed in the trucks as their drivers slowly headed back in the rain and fog. As the trucks were making their way to the LORAN Station, Wally thought he heard the engine whine and rotor noise from an HH-52. Wally asked his driver to please head down the taxi way to see if he was right.

1715

We manned Rescue-1425 for the return trip to LORAN Station Attu to pick up the other four survivors and return to Shemya. Smitty hooked up an external power cart to assist the weak battery for the engine start. I started the engine and engaged the rotors without incident as Jones re-familiarized himself with the HH-52 cockpit. He had never flown in a 52 with radar, so the cockpit configuration was a little different. He also had never flown with the LORAN C computer, so he watched as I set up the "go to" function for navigating from Shemya to Casco Cove.

I taxied away from the terminal and requested takeoff from the taxi way into the westerly wind. Jones remained silent as we lifted off and headed toward Attu. Weather was not abating; winds were still 20 knots out of the southwest, and the ceiling was still less than 300 feet with fog. I proceeded to Attu at 80 knots, between 70 and100 feet agl, staying south of the western Semechi Islands. I had to slow down to 40 knots as we came to Alexai Point. We had once again entered the "beehive" of bird activity, and Jones was wild eyed as I kept Rescue-1425 on a steady heading into Massacre Bay. I told him we had transited this way before and did not have a bird strike before...but it was very uncomfortable with the birds zooming and darting all around us.

Finally we cleared the bird area and continued toward the entrance to Casco Cove. The Angel Hole had disappeared; the visibility and ceiling had dropped significantly at the LORAN Station. Rescue-1425's radar was invaluable. Without it, we would have never been able to safely navigate in the existing conditions.

We pressed on, once we crossed the beachline, the runway appeared right on our nose. I flew down the west side of the runway and again button hooked to a landing into the wind on runway 200.

1800

I landed Rescue-1425 and shut the rotor down with the engine running as we awaited the arrival of the four survivors now nine hours and 31 minutes since the mishap. Smitty and I were shocked all the ambulatory survivors we had previously brought to the LORAN Station now had to be assisted or carried to the aircraft. Stevens and Sloboda were brought over in stretchers as Whyte and Van de Noort slowly walked with support by crewmen. Another vehicle drove up, Wally crawled out his wet suit discolored, covered in mud and soot. He slowly walked up to my side of Rescue-1425, he could see someone else wearing his helmet in the copilot seat. I greeted him and could see both confusion and exhaustion in his eyes. He was suffering from exhaustion and slightly hypothermic, shivering because the inside of his wet suit was cold-soaked with perspiration.

He still managed a broad smile and shook my outstretched hand. "Who's in my seat?"

Jones raised the face shield, and Wally immediately recognized him. "That helmet looks good on you, Commander," he said before providing us with an update on the search.

They had had no luck in finding SN Berryhill or any sign that anyone had walked away from the crash site. The fires had finally burned out; the weather had not gotten any better; and light was fading fast. We could tell Wally was totally exhausted; he was still taking deep breaths after the hour-and-a-half-long walk out to Murder Point.

"Wally, you can have your seat back," Jones spoke up, "and I will fly in the back with the survivors."

"No sir, please stay; I'm exhausted," Wally surprised me in saying. "I would not be any help in the cockpit in my condition."

On further discussion, we decided Wally would remain at Attu. He was now most familiar with the crash site and could continue to lead the ground searches the next morning. I was very concerned about leaving my affable copilot, but Wally felt it best, so I let it go.

After Smitty secured the stretchers and semi-ambulatory survivors in troop seats, Wally again stepped away from Rescue-1425 and gave me a thumbs up.

1822

I engaged the rotors of Rescue-1425 and was airborne from Casco Cove enroute Shemya. Even though sunset was four hours away, light was fading fast, and forward visibility was getting poor heading east. As we crossed the beachline and went feet wet (over water), the ever-present fog met us head on. I stayed clear of the "Birds" by flying further west toward Agattu Strait. We were flying at between 50 and 80 feet awl and at 80 knots, staying out of the clouds that still gripped the area. As we cleared Agattu Strait, Jones contacted the Shemya air controller, who said he had radar contact with us. Jones discussed with me on ICS about obtaining vectors from the Shemya controller for our final approach and landing. This would ease the burden of navigating on radar and having to slow down as we approached the islands ahead.

"Rescue-1425 is visual with the water at 70 feet," Jones told the controller; "Forward visibility is less than one half mile. Request vectors to final."

The Shemya controller rogered and immediately gave us a vector to the northeast. I looked at the radar and the proposed vector. It would have us fly directly into Alaid Island, which rises to 668 feet in less than a mile!

I immediately questioned the vector. "Shemya Approach Rescue-1425, that vector appears to take us directly into Alaid Island?"

"Roger overflight of the island," the controller stated. "I understand you are VFR."

The discussion deteriorated as I explained we were not VFR. We'd already told them we were flying at 70 feet above the water and had less than half mile forward visibility. The controller had not handled many helicopters flying in and out of Shemya at low level, so it was a stalemate.

I was fatigued and frustrated at this point, so I declined any further assistance. One mishap was enough for the day!

Jones and I discussed the recent fate of Rescue-1420 from CGAS Barbers Point, HI. That helo had been given a vector from a controller in bad weather and flew into the side of a cliff, killing all on board [LCDR Horton (Buzz) Johnson, LT Colleen Cain and AD2 David Thompson] on 7 January 1982. One of the last duties I performed at CGAS Port Angeles was to be a pall bearer for AD2 Dave Thompson's military funeral in Port Angeles. It was a very emotional day. Dave had been a crewman for the past three years at Port Angeles during my tenure. He was an outstanding crewman and individual. Not a dry eye was seen that day as Taps was blown at the funeral. With those sober facts fresh in our minds, Jones assisted me in piloting Rescue-1425 into Shemya on our own without incident.

1845

We safely landed and taxied to the operations terminal with the four survivors. Medical personnel ran out to take the rest of the survivors into the field hospital 10 hours and 16 minutes after the mishap. Jones and I breathed a sigh of relief as we took off our helmets, unstrapped, and climbed out of Rescue-1425. Jones said he was not sure how helpful he was especially with the controller vector snafu.

"Having you aboard gave me a big relief," I told him, "as I am really beat. I could have made a lot of mistakes, but since I was talking to you about every procedure, it kept me focused."

We walked back into the terminal, which was now teaming with medical personnel working on the survivors. I could see Kodiak Flight Surgeon, Dr. Marty Nemiroff with Michals. Word came Michals had to be defibrillated but was holding on and was stabilized.

Smitty and I had completed a more-than 11-hour crew day, with more than seven hours of flying Rescue-1425, since we launched on the morning fisheries patrol. I was overcome with emotions as I witnessed everyone receiving medical attention. I needed some air and quiet, so I walked out of the terminal and over to the riprap on the northwest side of the terminal area. I sat on a flat boulder and began to take in all I had witnessed that day; the miracle anyone survived the crash on the mountain; the miracle Scherrer found an Emergency Beacon and energized it; the miracle *Mellon* was so close and able to transit on turbines in those conditions and to refuel Rescue-1425 in nine minutes; the miracle we were close enough and able to fly in those conditions to rescue our shipmates; the miracle CG-1602 had been so close for the divert; the miracle the medevac personnel and aircraft had made it to Shemya and safely landed in poor weather; the miracle LORAN Station Attu and Air Force personnel were fit and able to assist on the rescue in a myriad of ways!

It was difficult to comprehend that a Coast Guard HC-130H had suffered such a horrific crash and most onboard had survived. My thoughts turned to what we had done in Rescue-1425 and how close we had come to the edge several times throughout the day. I almost lost it on the side of the mountain with the inadvertent pickling of the stabilization system... What a day!

My thoughts turned to the survivors who were not out of the woods yet, especially Michals and Young and to AE3 Canfield's loved ones and friends, for he was gone. Then my thoughts went to SN Berryhill. Was he alive or dead? Where was he? Had he walked away over the mountain? Was he OK? Could he survive in those conditions?

I sat on the rock, as tears rolled down my cheeks when all that came to mind was my pregnant wife expecting our first child back in Kodiak. It was a time for prayers and to release the emotions that overcame me. *Psalm 23* rushed to my consciousness and I said it out loud:

> *"The Lord is my shepherd, I shall not want. He maketh me to lie down in green pastures. He leadeth me beside the still waters. He restoreth my*

soul. He leadeth me in the path of righteousness for his name sake. Yeah, though I walk through the valley of the shadow of death, I will feel no evil, for thou art with me, thy rod and thy staff, they comfort me. Thou prepares a table before me in the presence of mine enemies. Thou anoitntest my head with oil, my cup runneth over. Surely goodness and mercy shall follow me all the days of my life, and I dwell in the house of the Lord forever."

My thoughts were calming down, and I knew it would be good to get home in a month or so.

1900

Suddenly someone was yelling for me to come into the terminal and see CDR Wright. Smitty and I were brought over to the makeshift operations area, where Hoover and Wright were on the phone. NORPACSARCOORD Juneau had postulated from survivor interviews that SN Berryhill had possibly gone over the ridge to the west further into the Weston Mountains, thinking he could find assistance. Since neither the wheeled nor track vehicles from the LORAN Station could make it into that area or even to the crash site because of the harsh terrain, Juneau wanted Rescue-1425 to return to Attu and conduct a night mountain search for him.

Smitty's and my face said it all. Ashen and white, we knew it was not possible to safely fly at night in the existing environmental conditions in that mountainous terrain. In those days, we had no **N**ight **V**ision **G**oggles (NVG) or specialized **F**orward **L**ooking **I**nfra-**R**ed (FLIR) system to help us search. Not that NVGs or FLIR would have worked in the existing conditions. Smitty and I were the only qualified HH-52 pilot and crew on Shemya. We were exhausted both physically and mentally and CDR Wright knew it.

Everyone at Shemya discussed the situation and all agreed it was not possible for any further searches especially a night sortie because the last section of 3710 guidance would apply: *"...**Probable loss of the (rescue) aircrew is not an acceptable risk.**"* Under the existing conditions that was a very real possibility. *Mellon* was also on the phone patch with NORPACSARCOORD Juneau, and they concurred the weather was getting worse and strongly recommended no night flights. *Mellon* would continue their beach patrols with motor surf boats until dark, and they would staff, with six volunteers from the station, a signal fire at Krasni Point all night. Station Attu personnel would bring some of their station dogs to assist if SN Berryhill was nearby. Further discussions ensued with NORPACSARCOORD Juneau that Smitty and I were not privy to but we heard "pound sand" and the abrupt hanging up of a phone.

NORPACSARCOORD Juneau continued to work the problem of finding SN Berryhill, if he had indeed survived and went the wrong way back into the interior of the mountain range. Arrangements were made for an Air Force Canine Search Team consisting of five dogs and handlers from McCord AFB, WA, to be flown by a CGAS Sacramento HC-130 to Kodiak and then a Kodiak HC-130 to Shemya AFB. The canine team would then be transported via helicopter to Attu to try and find SN Berryhill the next day.

1920

The survivors were stabilized and carefully loaded into the Air Force KC-135 medevac aircraft. Dr. Nemiroff wanted the fastest and smoothest ride for the patients which would be aboard the KC-135. The final miracle of the day was the survivors safely landing at Elmendorf AFB in Anchorage, AK, 18 hours after the mishap for advanced medical care. Anchorage is 1,478 nm from Attu, which is the same distance as Miami, FL, is from Denver, CO.

With the survivors' airborne heading to Anchorage, Smitty and I headed to the galley to eat. I kept an emergency $10 bill in my wet suit pocket, so we had money for the galley since all our personal gear including our wallets and military IDs were on *Mellon*. We knew we looked like hell with so much dirt, blood, and sweat caked on our wet suits. Our bright red wet suits had taken on a blackish hue from working at the crash site. We also smelled horrible because the wet suits were permeated with smoke and perspiration.

We scrubbed our hands and faces in the head (restroom) adjacent to the galley, which made us feel a bit better. I still had a dehydration headache that was eating at me. We ate together and became aware everyone in the galley was looking at us and whispering to each other, but no one spoke a word to us...it was uncomfortable and a bit creepy as the Air Force personnel just stared at us. The stares continued and it made Smitty and me wonder what were they thinking? We knew we had cheated death ourselves, but in the end we had done something few Coasties had ever done, which was rescue our own! We had done our jobs, and were totally exhausted both mentally and physically.

After eating the hot meal and rehydrating with several glasses of water and juice, my headache finally subsided, and we headed over to billeting. After getting our rooms, we both took long showers, no sea showers (wet body, turn off water, soap body, turn on water to rinse, turn off water), that day. I had been at sea for close to a month, so it felt as if the shower was moving, rocking slowly back and forth. This was something that always happened when returning home from an ALPAT as every room in the house seemed to be moving slightly especially when walking down a confined hallway or while in a small room like a bathroom. It took a while for the inner ear to stabilize from the constant shipboard movements.

As the hot water bathed me, I started to scrub my wet suit. The soot and mud flowed down the drain as my suit returned to its original red color. I peeled off the wet suit and turned it inside out to wash it out. Next was my Nomex® long underwear and finally I started on my body...wow being able to have a long hot shower, what a blessing. I just stood in the shower letting the warm water fall on my aching body and washing away the thoughts of the injuries to CG-1600 survivors, the death of Canfield and Berryhill, who was still missing on Attu.

I dug out my emergency shaving kit from my helmet bag for some deodorant and a tooth brush. Now feeling somewhat normal my thoughts still could not leave the nagging question of SN Berryhill, possibly on the mountain heading west away from the LORAN Station. I grabbed the last and only dry garment I had, a flight suit from the bottom of my helmet bag. I headed to the billeting office to borrow a fan, otherwise my wet suit and long underwear would still be wet in the morning. I turned my bathroom into a drying room for my wet suit and clothes. Totally fatigued, I tried to go to sleep. Sleep came hard; I kept thinking about the survivors, their serious injuries, and Juneau's night sortie request to find SN Berryhill if he was on the mountain trying to survive in those horrendous weather conditions...

Once at the LORAN Station, Wally compartmentalized his thoughts, thinking more about finding Berryhill than all the other activities of the day. Did Berryhill survive and walk up the side of the mountain in search of the LORAN Station? Why would he leave the crash site without talking to any other survivors? Was he disoriented and confused? Wally and the other ground search team members were hoping and praying he was alive and would be found soon.

Wally was totally dehydrated from the physically exhausting work in his wet suit on the mountain. After drinking some juice at the galley, he asked where he could shower and get out of his wet suit. Wilson led Wally to a bunk room and shower...Wally took a long hot shower, spending most of the time mustering up the strength to take off the wet suit. After peeling off his wet suit, he almost collapsed in the shower. He had no energy. Shutting off the water and toweling off took all the energy he had left. Feeling exhausted but clean Wally realized he had a wrapped towel around him but no clean clothes to wear. He sheepishly yelled for help, and some clothes were given to him in quick order.

Wally headed to the galley with the borrowed clothes for a little sustenance. He was not really hungry but knew he needed something. After eating a little, all Wally wanted was to get some sleep, but Wilson called to tell him NORPACSARCOORD Juneau was requesting Rescue-1425 fly back for a night search in the mountains. Wally had the same reaction as his crew did at Shemya.

"No way, it would be suicide in these conditions. No one could safely fly and search at night in that terrain in those conditions!"

LORAN Station Attu sent their recommendation of no helicopter night search, which was heeded. Wally was mentally and physically exhausted as he headed to bed. As always Wally got on his knees and asked God to protect his family, relatives, and friends, followed by a Hail Mary and an Our Father. On this particular night, however, he added special prayers for deceased crewmember Canfield and a further special request to help find

SN Berryhill. One last prayer was for his teammates....Bill and Smitty.

While lying in bed, Wally reflected on how little survival gear and clothing was found onsite, or how long it took to find it, but he was benevolent for finding size 9 boots to replace his well-worn and torn wet suit booties. Wally knew the next day could be a long and busy one. Sleep came fast (as it always did) for him.

Fog and rain shroud crash site day of rescue. Looks like an underwater photo of CG-1600 tail section. Wallace collection.

Clearer picture from same vantage point next day.
Wallace collection.

Late afternoon photo of part of crash site in fog.
Wallace collection.

Upper crash site survivor shelter area note wing panel, life raft,
and survival suit lower left side. USCG photo.

Sight picture from cockpit of HH-52 for landing aboard ship.
USCG photo.

CG-1425 landing aboard *Mellon* earlier on ALPAT.
Peterson collection.

USAF KC-135 medevac aircraft. USAF photo.

Chapter 6

NO ONE LEFT BEHIND

"For whoever wants to save their life will lose it, but whoever loses their life for me will save it."

Luke 9:24

0530 31 July 1982

Next morning came all too quickly and while having breakfast with the station crew, Wally could sense the collective pride of what they had accomplished the previous day, without having spoken a word....the minimal chatter they had was focused on the days goal: to find SN Berryhill.

It was a restless sleep for Smitty and me at Shemya AFB. I met Smitty at the galley for breakfast at 0545. We had planned for a 0645 launch back to Attu to search for SN Berryhill. I recalled with Smitty the WWII Battle for Attu referencing that Captain Willoughby and 244 of his Scout Battalion were dropped off from the submarines **NUTILUS** and **NARWAHAL** in Austin Cove on the western side of Attu Island. Their job was to hike to the snow-filled ridgelines of the mountains eastward to close the backdoor on the assault in Holtz Bay. Willoughby and his men had to climb the coastal cliff area and then traverse across the island in the muskeg and snow for five days with only one and a half day's rations. They were not dressed for the conditions they encountered. His men prevailed in the cold wind, fog, and snow that besieged them.[51] If Willoughby and his men could survive and then go into battle, maybe SN Berryhill had a chance.

Smitty and I finished our breakfast, grabbed our helmet bags, and headed to Base Ops for a weather brief, as we were already in our wet suits ready for our next flight. Weather was not good as we made our way to Base Ops; winds were still 15 to 20 knots, visibility was less than a mile, and the ceiling looked to be less than 400 feet. I was able to get on an HF radio and talked directly with *Mellon* anchored in Temnac Bay just west of Krasni Point. *Mellon* report on-scene weather as wind 205 at 20 knots, visibility one half nm in rain and fog, ceiling was overcast at 200 feet, and temperature was 50 degrees Fahrenheit. It did not look good for a first light sortie.

0630
No luck at the signal fire that night; SN Berryhill remained missing. LORAN Station Attu was sending out three land parties to search the crash site, and *Mellon* intended to launch its small boat to resume searching the beachline areas. Smitty and I headed out to preflight Rescue-1425 so we could launch when weather allowed.

After searching the main wreckage for about 30 minutes, a LORAN Station search team found SN Berryhill dead under some metal debris not more than ten feet from where Wally had cut apart a parachute to cover AM3 Weise the day before. He had died on impact, just as AT3 Canfield had, but he was badly burned by the subsequent fire and hidden from view under a large metal piece of CG-1600's cabin. The sad news was passed that all personnel aboard CG-1600 were accounted for and no one had walked away from the accident into the mountains as previously thought. It was a sobering fact Berryhill did not make it; we now had two Coast Guard fatalities. We were grieving for the loss, but we also felt a huge relief in not launching the previous night because it would not have made a difference...the right call was made under the conditions but a haunting one for me. *Mellon* recovered their small boat and reported the fog was lifting and visibility was increasing.

0900

Mellon reported visibility had increased to five nm and the ceiling was at least 400 feet. Shemya AFB was also experiencing better weather, so I was cleared to fly to LORAN Station Attu to pick up Wally and the two deceased personnel. Smitty and I headed to CG-1425 for the flight to Attu.

0915

The Air Force ground crew came up to Smitty and told him the pilot of the helicopter needed to come back into Base Ops for an important phone call. I unstrapped from the cockpit and headed back into to Base Ops. It was the CGAS Kodiak duty officer telling me my rescue crew was to be relieved of duty on *Mellon* and to return to CGAS Kodiak that day aboard a CGAS Kodiak HC-130 which was enroute to Shemya. We were being relieved to be interviewed by the investigation boards (Mishap/Safety and Administrative) that would be arriving in Kodiak. Replacement pilots and plane captain would be on the plane, and we were to plan for a 1700 local departure from Shemya. I was surprised at the decision but understood. I rogered all and told Smitty what was up.

0945

Smitty and I resumed our launch and flew at 300 feet to Attu. We flew toward Krasni Point enroute to Casco Cove but could not make out the crash site on the mountain because of the low ceiling. We flew into the LORAN Station, landed, and shutdown. Wilson and Wallace met us on shutdown to discuss the situation. It was a difficult time. Wilson had lost one of his crewmen, and another was in the hospital at Anchorage with significant injuries. I explained we had been ordered to fly back to Kodiak that afternoon, so we would take the deceased in body bags with us and on the HC-130 back to Kodiak.

Wally and I could not thank Wilson enough for his crew's outstanding actions during the rescue. Wilson said all his crew talked about was how the helicopter aircrew pushed them to their limits on the mountain.

"Hopefully, they didn't take our urgings wrong," Wally and I told him. "They did a tremendous job. It couldn't have been done without their efforts." In particular, the five crewmen that flew with me and brought down the critically injured survivors must have thought I was a mad man flying alone in that weather."

"Let's just say in the end they were impressed," the CO said. "You guys really did a tremendous job in horrible conditions."

Wally thanked Wilson again for the hospitality, clothes, and the bed for the night. Then Wally, Smitty, and I helped load the body bags and our rescue basket into CG-1425. It was the last time anyone of us landed again at Casco Cove until I, as the new CGAS Kodiak Operations Officer, flew on an HC-130H Attu logistics flight in October of 1993. Not much had changed; Casco Cove still did not have any navigational aids. However improved radars and global positioning systems (GPS) lowered the risk factors considerably.

1050

CG-1425 was airborne with our complete crew and Wally at the pilot's controls enroute to Shemya. I raised *Mellon* on 381.8 and explained we had been ordered back to Kodiak for the investigation boards. New pilots and plane captain from CGAS Kodiak were enroute now to Shemya. We planned to return to pack our personal gear, debrief, and return to Shemya for the flight back to Kodiak.

It was not a well-received message on *Mellon* because the AVDET and *Mellon* crew had formed a very special bond. We had earned each other's trust and admiration through the professionalism and determination displayed during the deployment and specifically in the execution of the SAR case. With the rescue phase over, *Mellon* was ordered to remain at Attu to assist the investigation boards that were being set up by Coast Guard District 17 and Coast Guard Headquarters. I told *Mellon* we would return around 1400.

1120

Our flight to Shemya was uneventful as weather steadily improved. We landed and taxied in abeam Base Ops. Shemya ground personnel assisted us in removing the body bags with the deceased and taking them to a secure holding place at the terminal. Wally, Smitty, and I headed to the galley for an early lunch and to talk...it was the first time we could talk about what had happened the previous day.

In 1982, the Coast Guard had not begun critical incident stress management debriefings, but we knew we needed to talk and get things off our chests and clear our minds of what we had done.

"I thought we were going to hit all those birds coming into Attu," Smitty recalled, "and that you had crashed when the wind gust blew you off the mountain."

Wally chimed in. "Yes, those birds were unbelievable; I can't believe we didn't hit any! I knew you hadn't crashed, one, we didn't hear anything except the wind blowing; and two, I knew you could handle it"

"I grabbed the cyclic so hard," I sheepishly confessed. "That gust caught me so off guard I disengaged ASE. I was asshole and elbows until I reengaged ASE and was able to slow everything down...it was like time stopped. I was able to work through the big three Aviate, Navigate, and then Communicate! I missed you as my copilot Wally, but I think the good Lord took your seat and kept me out of trouble."

They smiled and chuckled a little at my statement, but they knew it was a miracle I didn't crash Rescue-1425 in those conditions.

"All those hours hovering ASE off on the taxiway at Kodiak paid off!" Wally said.

"Yes they did," I said. "It really did help me."

I asked about the crash site because I had not seen much of it. Wally and Smitty both shared their impressions.

"It was total devastation."

"It was amazing anyone could have survived the crash."

"The ground was so steep and uneven."

"The impact marks were huge; it wasn't like they lightly touched down and slid up the mountain."

"The fuel fires burned for a long time. I was surprised only one survivor was burned."

"There wasn't much left, especially of the survival gear. They wouldn't have made it on the mountain much longer."

"Whyte and Scherrer did a lot, but hypothermia would have most likely killed the severely injured because they had very little shelter from the elements."

Then Wally said "I took some pictures while on scene with my little camera I carry on all flights. They should be amazing pictures if they turn out."

"You guys did a great job readying the survivors to get them off the mountain," I told them. "What you did was nothing short of amazing!"

Smitty and Wally echoed the same to me...it was a team effort, and we worked well together.

Then I told Wally about *Mellon*.

"*Mellon* did a super job in getting close to Krasni Point, refueling us, and getting us back airborne in 9 minutes! They have the best flight deck crew and CIC that I have ever seen."

Wally and Smitty agreed they were the best crew they had seen on ALPAT. We talked about the loss of two, which was a sobering fact, but nine had survived, which was astounding. *Mellon* being so close and able to launch the helo to get them to advanced medical care from such a remote site...just how lucky can one get? The decompression worked as our discussion subsided, and we finished our lunch in the silence of personal reflection.

1320

We went over to Base Ops and found out the HC-130 from Kodiak was due in at 1600 local, which was a little later than the original planned arrival time. We headed back out to CG-1425 for our final trip to *Mellon*. Shemya weather was clearing; visibility was ten nm, ceiling was between 800 and 1000 feet, and the winds were 220 at ten knots. It was great weather to fly in. We took off and flew directly to *Mellon*, anchored in Temnac Bay near Krasni Point.

As we approached *Mellon*, we could, for the first time make out the crash site on the side of the mountain. Smitty used the helicopter camera to snap some pictures as we flew by just offshore, the first overhead pictures of the crash site. It was an amazing sight to be able to see the extent of the crash on the side of the mountain. We were awestruck at the size of the debris field and crash site. None of us imagined the length and size of the debris field and burned area. For the first time, we could see the distances we hovered to get to the crash site for the rescue from

Murder Point. It was a sobering sight...then waves of the persistent Aleutian fog engulfed the crash site, and we could see it no more.

1356

I landed CG-1425 uneventfully on *Mellon*. We took primary tie-downs and secured the engine and rotors. Wally and Smitty huddled with the rest of our aircrew (Hissom, Hassinger, and Jordan) to explain what was going on AVDET-wise. I headed to the bridge to discuss the orders to return to Kodiak and was met with some resistance from *Mellon* senior leadership, who wanted to discuss the order with CGAS Kodiak via a phone patch. I explained that, unfortunately, this was standard practice, and protests might be taken in the wrong light because CGAS Kodiak had just had a change of command days before the mishap. A new CO was at Kodiak with a mishap right after he took over, it was a difficult time.

I had discussed with Wally on the flight to *Mellon* we should request to come back on the deployment after we provided our statements to the boards. I passed that to Daniell and Sabo, who were happy we might be able to rendezvous with them in a week or so. Wally, Smitty, and I retrieved and loaded our personal gear in CG-1425. The flight deck was full, with most of the *Mellon* crew not on watch saying their goodbyes. I was torn. I really was not ready to leave *Mellon* and the rest of my AVDET. We had a great AVDET, and I felt like I was abandoning them and *Mellon*. The remaining AVDET (Hissom, Hassinger, and Jordan) would need to integrate with the new plane captain and pilots, after what we had been through, would take some effort.

1615

We made what was to be our last deployment takeoff from *Mellon* and headed to Shemya. Thirty minutes later, we arrived at Shemya and taxied to our now reserved spot by Base Ops. The replacement crew met us and began to haze us, I cut them off. It may have been funny to them, but we weren't in the mood for that kind of banter. I explained, in no uncertain terms, we did not want to go back to Kodiak and be replaced. Wally, Smitty, and I were committed to this deployment and did not want anyone replacing us. I explained that we knew *Mellon* was planning on a refuel stop at Naval Base Adak in eight to ten days and we would request to be there to resume the deployment.

With the transfer of CG-1425 completed, Wally, Smitty, and I loaded our gear on the Kodiak HC-130 and checked to ensure the recovered remains of Canfield and Berryhill were also on board. We strapped into the troop seats in the cargo hold of the HC-130. It would be a long and somber 7-hour flight back to CGAS Kodiak.

Chapter 7

HEALING AND RECOVERY

"For I know the plans I have for you, says the Lord, plans for welfare and not for evil, to give you a future and a hope. Then you will call upon me and come and pray to me, and I will hear you."

Jeremiah 29:11-12

CAPT Martin Nemiroff, Chief Medical Officer at Coast Guard Support Center Kodiak, led the medical team that had been treating CG-1600 survivors for over eight hours when the Air Force KC-135 medevac jet landed at Elmendorf AFB. It was just after midnight in Anchorage when the hospital bus and ambulance pulled up to the jet. It only took 12 minutes for the Air Force medical personnel to load the survivors for transport. COL Evan Griffith, Commander of the 21st Tactical Fighter Wing at Elmendorf, watched in silence as the injured crewmen of CG-1600 were loaded.

"There are seldom any survivors when a plane as large as a C-130 goes down," he commented to reporters on scene. "These people are damn lucky to be alive."[52]

Michals was rushed by ambulance to Providence hospital critical care facility because of his extensive burns and spinal injuries. The rest of the survivors were transported to Elmendorf AFB Hospital's newly opened intensive care wing. CAPT Nemiroff was physically and mentally spent. He had been up for more than 18 hours, flown more than 14 hours that day 2,600 nm from Kodiak to Attu and then from Attu to Anchorage, tended to the survivors for more than eight hours, and assisted in the transfer of the survivors to the hospital staff.[53]

Commander Mike Stenger, the Executive Officer (XO) at Air Station Kodiak, was instrumental in coordinating a special Coast Guard HC-130 flight from Kodiak to Elmendorf for the wives and loved ones. On arriving at the Elmendorf Hospital, most of CG-1600 crew were met by their wives and loved ones. Whyte remembers his wife Marjorie, a registered nurse, was allowed to sit with him while he received stiches to his head wounds.[54] Coast Guard Chaplain CDR Ed Gates had flown over from Kodiak, and he met with all the survivors especially the single crew members. CDR Gates commented that all survivors were in relatively good spirits and "They are very glad to be alive."[55]

By Saturday morning, everyone at Elmendorf Hospital had received primary treatments and was resting. Several were scheduled for orthopedic surgeries that would come once swelling had subsided. COL Warren Carpenter, Commander of Elmendorf Hospital, spoke to reporters and was very optimistic about the patient's recovery

"There is no serious threat now. There were some fractures-- legs, arms, ribs, ankles--but no serious burns among the patients here (Elmendorf AFB Hospital). We expected some internal injuries but have not found any."[56]

AT3 Michals remained in critical condition at Providence Hospital Thermal Unit with severe burns and spinal cord damage.

Like the mythological Phoenix which, after a long life, dies in a fire of its own making only to rise again from the ashes, many of the survivors of CG-1600 would need to rise from the ashes. Their injuries would be both physiological and psychological. Several would take years to recover, and others would be able to move forward in a short amount of time. Seven of the survivors would continue in the Coast Guard and complete full careers. Two of the survivors had to be medically retired and would have significant physical challenges ahead of them.

Virginia Van den Noort was the first survivor to be released after 2 days of observation. She had suffered some bruising, soreness, and shock but no fractures or internal injuries.

The next to be released were Whyte, Scherrer, and Sloboda, who flew back from Anchorage on CG-1602 Tuesday 3 August. Approximately 75 Coast Guard personnel met the aircraft at CGAS Kodiak to welcome home the three survivors.[57]

Whyte, PIC, was in a thigh-to-ankle cast for his cracked knee cap for six weeks and was able to return to flight status after two more months of rehabilitation at Kodiak.[58]

Scherrer, Copilot, recovered from his broken nose and cracked ribs in three weeks and was able to return to flight status in one and a half months at Kodiak.[59]

Sloboda, Flight Engineer, recovered from his broken arm and wrist in six weeks and was able to return to flight status inside of two months.[60]

Weise, Loadmaster, went through several surgeries and received rods, pins, and screws to stabilize his fractured left leg and ankle. He was at Elmendorf AFB Hospital for more than two weeks before being transported back to Kodiak for his transfer to CGAS Elizabeth City, NC. The Attu log mission was to be his final flight at CGAS Kodiak before he left the Island. His wife had already departed to Montana and had to be flown back to Kodiak to reunite with Dave. They made their way across country to CGAS Elizabeth City, where he received more medical treatments and physical therapy at Norfolk Naval Hospital. He remained in a leg cast for six months. His rehabilitation took three more months because his left leg was severely atrophied. Weise would ride his bicycle 20 miles round trip to work each day to get in shape. In June of 1983, he passed his flight physical and returned to full flight duties.[61]

Crocker, Dropmaster, went through several surgeries to implant a rod in his left tibia and plates and pins in his right ankle. He was in the Elmendorf AFB Hospital for three weeks and then transported to Maine by a military medevac aircraft. He spent several months rehabilitating at his parents'. In December of 1982, he reported to his new duty station CGAS Cape Cod. He passed his flight physical in 1983 and returned to flight status.[62]

Michals, Navigator, stayed at the Thermal Unit at Providence Hospital in Anchorage, strapped to a Styker frame for stabilization as his burns were being treated. It was an agonizing time as he was rotated in the frame and they treated his burns to prevent infection and further loss to his severely burned hands. The fingers on his left had to be amputated along with his right thumb. His neck was in traction during the agonizing burn treatments. One bright spot was the CGAS Kodiak Hangar 4 softball team, which played their hearts out for him. We took second in the state tournament, losing a close final game. The second place trophy was given to Michals at Providence and remained in his room throughout his stay, reminding him we all cared for him. An attempt was made to transfer him to the Brooks Army Medical Facility Burn unit in San Antonio, TX, but, after takeoff from Anchorage in the medevac aircraft, Michals suffered a respiratory arrest that required an immediate return to Providence Hospital. Michals stayed at Providence for numerous skin grafts and a bone graft to stabilize his neck. Michals suffered from paraplegia and was in Providence for over 3 months before his transfer to the Palo Alto Veterans Administration Spinal Cord Injury Center.[63]

Young, Radioman, experienced similar back and spinal cord injuries as Michals, caused by the extreme whiplash during the mishap. Young remained at the Elmendorf hospital longer than any other survivor to stabilize his spine. He suffered from paraplegia and was initially transferred to Seattle Veteran's Administration Hospital for treatment. After a short stay, he was transferred to the Palo Alto Veterans Administration Spinal Cord Injury Center.[64]

Stevens, new Attu crewman, was stabilized at Elmendorf Hospital. He went through orthopedic surgery to implant a rod in his badly broken arm. His eyesight was fully restored after his eyes were swollen shut for four days. Fortunately, the impact of the flying object did not break any facial bones. He received compression factures of T4-7 vertebrae but was able to recover. Stevens was flown to Support Center Kodiak for several months of rest and rehabilitation before he returned to LORAN Station Attu to complete his unaccompanied tour of duty.[65]

The Aviation Safety Mishap (MAB) and Administrative Investigation Boards met separately with the crew from CG-1600 and Rescue-1425. Smitty, Wally, and I met with the Mishap Analysis Board (MAB) first, and found it an interesting dialog. The MAB was focused on why CG-1600 crashed. They were primarily interested in the exact location of the mishap, location of the survivors and deceased, location of the wreckage with respect to major parts, anything that could lead them to facts, findings, and recommendations to preclude future mishaps.

The MAB found it hard to believe my crew and I did not know or see more than we did. Smitty and Wally were able to offer a lot more information on the crash site because they were on-scene with the survivors and interacting more than I. Our brief overhead observation of the crash site when returning to *Mellon* before our departure to Kodiak provided the only crash scene perspective. We did not know why or how CG-1600 crashed on the side of the mountain. All we knew and told them was "It was a miracle anyone survived."

Several of the MAB members were skeptical of what we told them, especially questioning the steepness of the incline and that the only large piece of the airframe left was the empennage (tail) section, which was facing 180 degrees from the crash direction. How was that possible? The Administrative Board members were more accepting of what we told them, and, appropriately, they were very interested in documenting the success of all the players that assisted in rescuing CG-1600's survivors.

The weather at Attu precluded any flights for the board members for over a week, so they were able to interview survivors in Anchorage and then again in Kodiak, until the weather cleared. Ten days after the mishap, the weather relented, and the boards finally made it to Attu. They could see firsthand the devastating crash site and experience for themselves the arduous task of climbing to and around the crash site. The reality of what we attempted to explain days before unfolded before them...it truly was a miracle that anyone had survived.

The board members had to literally piece together the crash, with debris spread out over an area covering two football fields. It was a daunting task for the members of the investigation teams. Many recommendations and observations from the mishap were used to improve the HC-130 equipment and operations. The Boards addressed many recommendations from Rescue-1425 experience to enhance future rescues operations.

After the MAB returned to CGAS Kodiak, one board member found his way to my house on base to offer his apology for not believing what my crew and I had told him. He could not imagine what we had told him and the conditions we described as factual until he hiked in from Murder Point to the crash site. The old adage of "Seeing is believing" came to fruition for the investigators. It took until late February of 1983 for the Mishap Investigation with final actions to be completed.

After the mishap, a CGAS Kodiak wide flight safety stand-down was initiated for all the aircrews to wrap their heads around what had just occurred. The U.S. Navy Special Psychiatric Rapid Intervention Team (SPRINT) from Naval Medical Center Portsmouth, VA, was requested by the XO. After CG-1471 crashed, the SPRINT Team had come to CGAS Kodiak and proved to be a valuable resource. Stenger knew they would prove most useful again. (Note the Coast Guard now uses the CG CSID team for this interface)

They arrived two days later to begin the process of healing. The team provided short-term mental health and emotional support immediately following the mishap. The goal was to prevent long-term medical psychiatric dysfunction or disability. The team is composed of psychiatrists, psychologists, psychiatric nurses and nurse practitioners, licensed clinical social workers, Navy Chaplains, Navy neuropsychiatric technicians, and civilian and U. S. Public Health Service personnel assigned to Navy Medical Center Portsmouth.[66]

The SPRINT Team proved most valuable because the loss of an HC-130H was unheard of in the Coast Guard. CG-1600 was the first CG C-130 to be lost since they came to the service in 1959. CGAS Kodiak, especially the aircrew families, needed to talk through the mishap. It was the first time I had experienced this type of intervention. Smitty, Wally, and I went over the rescue with SPRINT team members, and we were flagged as traumatized by the events but not in distress. This was a valuable lesson Wally and I took with us as we ascended to higher positions in Coast Guard aviation. Rescuers can and will become traumatized and possibly suffer from **P**ost-**T**raumatic **S**tress **D**isorder (PTSD). I had many a sleepless night of nightmares and flashbacks of this rescue and others in my career. PTSD is very real and it can haunt both rescuers and survivors alike especially when others have been badly injured or died.

True to our word, at the eight day mark, Wally and I requested to return to *Mellon* to complete our AVDET as *Mellon* was scheduled to refuel at Naval Station Adak. The request was denied by the Command. We were disappointed, as was *Mellon*. Wally and I continued to fly together whenever we could, but we were told we would not deploy together again because we were needed to break-in the new pilots and assist them in obtaining their Alaskan Aircraft Commander designations for ALPAT deployments.

Chapter 8

THE REST OF THE STORY

"Our Father, who art in heaven, hallowed by thy name, thy kingdom come, thy will be done, on earth as it is in heaven. Give us this day our daily bread; and forgive us our trespasses, as we forgive those who trespass against us: and lead us not into temptation, but deliver us from evil. For thine is the kingdom, and the power, and the glory, forever and ever. Amen "

Matthew 6:9-13

CG-1600

AT3 Brad Canfield and SN Steven Berryhill died upon impact at 0830 on Friday 30 July 1982. Their bodies were recovered, and they were buried in their hometowns by their loved ones.

Stevens completed his isolated tour of duty at Attu without incident. He made several trips up to Weston Mountain during his time on Attu and wondered how it was he and the others had survived! Stevens continued his service in the Coast Guard as a machinist mate for 20 years, retiring in 1994. He currently works and resides in Terre Haute, Indiana.[67]

Whyte continued to fly HC-130s and the G-1 at CGAS Sacramento and Elizabeth City, respectfully, until he left flight status in 1989 because of medical reasons. He remained a staff officer at CGAS Elizabeth City until he retired after 20 years of service in 1991. Whyte and his family relocated back to Sacramento, CA, where he completed his degree in management and worked for the State of California after retiring from the Coast Guard. He and his wife of 43 years raised two children and are retired living in Sacramento.[68]

Scherrer continued to fly HC-130 for the Coast Guard until his retirement after 20 years of service. Scherrer continued to fly commercial aircraft in Alaska after leaving the Coast Guard.

Sloboda continued his career flying in HC-130s as a flight engineer until his retirement from the Coast Guard. He is retired and living in Florida.[69]

Weise continued to fly HC-130s as a loadmaster until 1989, when he completed HC-130 Flight Engineer School and training. Weise flew two more tours at CGAS Kodiak, and his first missions on returning to Kodiak were Attu log flights! On the 20th anniversary of the mishap, 30 July 2002, AM1 Weise flew an Attu log flight that culminated in a small celebration at the crash site. The LORAN Station crew went with Weise to the crash site on unit four-wheelers. Weise returned to CGAS Clearwater in 2005 where he retired in January 2010. He served 30 years in the Coast Guard, with more than 6,000 flight hours in Coast Guard HC-130 aircraft. He currently lives in Florida with his wife of 27 years. They raised two boys; his youngest is a Coast Guard aircrewman flying on HC-130s out of CGAS Clearwater, FL.[70]

Crocker completed his tour of duty at CGAS Cape Cod and also served two more tours of duty in Kodiak. He retired from the Coast Guard in 2000 at CGAS Clearwater. Crocker was married in 1985 and raised two boys. He currently works and lives in Maine with his wife of 21 years.[71]

Michals, with the support of his wife Wenda and his family, continued to receive inpatient rehabilitation and plastic surgeries at the Palo Alto VA for another seven months. In April 1983, he formally received his medical retirement from the Coast Guard. Michals medical challenges continue to this day from the injuries he sustained at Attu. He tried to go back to college but decided it wasn't for him and became a travel agent with his wife. It was something they could do together, and they enjoyed the perks of traveling all over. Craig and Wenda ran a successful travel business for 15 years. They decided they wanted children and began an adoption journey that few have experienced. They adopted their first child, a boy, in 1989. To date they have raised five children, four boys and a girl, ages 27 to 17, and has one granddaughter. Michals and his family in 2005/06 timeframe provided assistance to Hurricane Katrina survivors through their church by rebuilding homes and helping people rebuild their lives. Operating out of Bay St. Louis, MS. Craig was the designated driver in a modified van, his family helped in any way they could at the job sites. "It was the most rewarding work our family could do," Craig said. "Helping others in their time of need." It was the same purpose Craig set out to accomplish when he first enlisted in the Coast Guard: "Serving others".[72]

Young (now Devlin-Young) spent months of countless medical procedures and evaluations of his back and spinal injuries. Unfortunately, he suffered from irreversible paraplegia and was medially discharged from the Coast Guard. With his spine stabilized, Young began his rehabilitation at a the same Palo Alto, VA, rehab center as Michals, close to his home and family. Young was not happy as a young man suffering from paraplegia and living in a wheel chair. He would describe himself as a "bitter and angry." He was asked to be one of five participants at the First National Disabled Veterans Winter Sports Clinic. He credits that experience with changing his life. He was able to find a new focus, confidence and determination not just survive, but thrive in the challenges and to help others do the same.

"My goal is to help those with disabilities to realize their potential," said Devlin-Young. "Adaptive sports pushed me to be healthy -- mentally and physically -- and to stay in front of the ravages of the disability."

Today, he continues to train and compete on slopes around the world. But, unlike many elite athletes, when he's not skiing, this former California surf boy focuses on giving back to others by removing barriers for disabled athletes and making snow sports more accessible for the disabled.

"Skiing is a gravity-powered sport, so it's the Great Equalizer. In my wheelchair, I encounter dozens of obstacles every day. But on the snow, I just glide over it. There is so much freedom to be found. Learn a sport, get outside and play. The troubles of the disability will fade into the background. They aren't going to disappear-- but they will fade."

So, dedicated to helping others, Devlin-Young took 2 years off from racing himself to found and run the New England Adaptive Ski Team (NEDST) at Loon Mountain, NH, with his wife, Donna (a former elite ski racer). The couple quickly filled their ranks and coached three athletes to compete in the U.S. National Championships and on to the U.S. Adaptive Ski Team, where they won multiple World, Paralympic and World Cup medals. The NEDST at Loon was also instrumental in the creation of the Golden Cup series of races, named in honor of Devlin-Young's teammate, the legendary Diana Golden, who died of cancer. Delvin-Young's skiing achievements have been remarkable, spanning the past decade:

- ➤ 2015: Gold medal, Mono Skier X -- Winter X-games
- ➤ 2013: 3rd, World Cup Downhill Overall
- ➤ 2013: Gold medal, World Cup/Pre-Paralympic Downhill -- Sochi, Russia
- ➤ 2011: Gold medal, Super G, World Championships -- Sestriere, Italy
- ➤ 2010: 4th, Super G; 6th, Super Combined -- Paralympic Games--Vancouver, Canada
- ➤ 2010: 2nd, Super G -- World Cup--Sestriere, Italy
- ➤ 2008: 1st, World Cup Super G Overall (Eight podium finishes)
- ➤ 2008: Bronze medal, Mono-cross -- Winter X Games
- ➤ 2006: Gold, Mono-cross Winter X Games
- ➤ 2006: Silver medal, Downhill -- 2006 Paralympic Winter Games--Torino, Italy
- ➤ 2006: 1st, World Cup Super G Overall (second place in overall standings)
- ➤ 2005: Gold medal, Mono-cross -- Winter X Games
- ➤ 2005: 1st, World Cup Super G Overall (3 wins)
- ➤ 2005: 2nd, World Cup Giant Slalom Overall (5 wins).

Delvin-Young has found the same rewarding work: "Helping others in their time of need," which was his intent when he enlisted in the Coast Guard.[73]

The Rescuers

LORAN Station Attu's crew performed in an exceptional manner in conducting search and rescue operations for CG-1600. It was an all hands effort for the 24 man Coast Guard crew and the 10 visiting USAF personnel. LTJG Wilson and CWO Beard, Station CO and XO, provided outstanding leadership throughout the two day ordeal. Wilson integrated the USAF personnel into his teams to maximize their effectiveness. Many of crew searched throughout the day in arduous conditions of relentless wind and rain on the side of mountain. Others tended to the survivors that were brought to the Station by Rescue-1425. Of special note Technical Sargent (TSgt/E-6) Masuo, a senior medic from Shemya AFB, treated and tended to the four survivors brought to the Station until we could medevac them to Shemya several hours later.

Station personnel alongside *Mellon* personnel manned signal fires all night in hopes of finding SA Berryhill alive. On 31 July, one of three first light search parties consisting mainly of Station personnel found the remains of SA Berryhill at the crash site. LORAN Station Attu personnel preformed their duties in a selfless manner trying to save and find their shipmates on Weston Mountain.[74]

Mellon's crew received a Meritorious Unit Commendation from VADM C. E. Larkin, Commander, Coast Guard Pacific Area for the rescue of CG-1600. The citation read:

> *"For meritorious service from 30 July to 1 August 1982 while engaged in the rescue of the survivors of Coast Guard HC-130 1600 which crashed on Attu Island mountains in the vicinity of Murder Point the morning of 30 July 1982. Upon being notified by Communications Station Kodiak that the HC-130 1600 was overdue on a flight from Shemya Air Force Base to Attu Island LORAN Station, Mellon recovered her helicopter which was airborne on a coordinated law enforcement mission and proceeded to scene. Despite visibilities as low as one quarter mile in rain and fog Mellon proceeded on turbines at twenty-five knots from her initial*

position approximately 110 nautical miles east of Attu. Racing through the low Aleutian weather, the Mellon crew planned for the launch and coordinated search by helicopter and three fixed wing aircraft including a Coast Guard HC-130, a U.S. Air Force RC-135, and a Navy P-3. As on scene commander...The efforts of Mellon for a thirty-one hour period in coordinating and communicating the activities some 1400 miles from where anxious families and shipmates waited for information were outstanding. Their actions materially assisted the successful location, evacuation and treatment of the injured survivors.

The outstanding initiative, planning, performance, and unwavering devotion to duty displayed by Mellon personnel are in keeping with the highest traditions of the United States Coast Guard.

The Operational Distinguishing Device is authorized."[75]

Mellon transited 10,989.9 nm during the 60-day ALPAT (10 July-8 Sept). *Mellon* participated in 45 AVDET sorties, culminating in 73.7 flight hours. In addition to the rescue of CG-1600, *Mellon* participated in three additional SAR cases: The fishing vessel *Pacific Rose*, the medevac of a crewman to St. Paul Island, and a fire on board the 136-foot processor *Jeffron* off Unalaska. *Mellon* conducted 15 at-sea boarding and inspections of FFVs in support of the Magnuson Fishery Conservation and Management Act. It was an ALPAT they would not forget. It is not by coincidence the leadership team on *Mellon* was successful in their Coast Guard careers.[76]

CAPT Martin H. Daniell rose to the rank of VADM and served as Commander Pacific Area and Vice Commandant of the Coast Guard. Daniell retired after 36 years of service in 1994.

"This case was a challenge unique in my experience," he said of the rescue of CG-1600. "As On Scene Commander, I was in charge of the overall operation while LT Peterson's helicopter would perform the actual rescues. My most important role was to decide when to launch the helicopter; keeping in mind the prescribed operating envelope designed to provide for safe recovery of the helicopter should it encounter problems, and the imperative to arrive on scene quickly to save as many lives as possible. Once the helicopter had been launched, *Mellon* proceeded through limited visibility to a position off Attu Island, where she could provide support to the helicopter.

A critical part of this was landing the helicopter with a load of injured and refueling it in record time for its further transit to Shemya for medical treatment. Alaska and particularly the Western Aleutian Islands pose a unique operating environment. There are virtually no navigational aids, charts are unreliable, and the weather is consistently challenging. That this case had an unquestionably positive outcome is a tribute to the skill of the helicopter crew and to the teamwork of the *Mellon* crew who supported them. I am proud to have been a part of this all-hands effort."[77]

LT Jim Sabo rose to the rank of Captain (CAPT/06) and was CO of three Coast Guard cutters: *Alert* (WMEC-630), *Vigorous* (WMEC-627), and *Jarvis* (WHEC-725). CAPT Sabo ended his career serving as the First Commander of Coast Guard Patrol Forces Southwest Asia in the Kingdom of Bahrain. In that capacity, he was responsible for all Coast Guard Forces assigned to the Navy's Fifth Fleet in the Arabian Gulf during the Second Gulf War, Iraqi Freedom. CAPT Sabo retired after 30 years in the Coast Guard and then served as a Magistrate for the State of Virginia until 2015.

"Upon reflection on the CG-1600 operation over 30 years later," he said, "I believe there was a coming together of too many factors to be considered coincidence. Call it fate, luck, or divine intervention, but *Mellon*, with the personnel involved, became the right tool, at the right time, and in the right place to successfully prosecute this mission.

Mellon's key personnel were all either apprentice or journeyman sailors. We all, however, had two things in common: we had all been together for a year and had been trained by the best true Alaskan Sailor, CAPTAIN Martin Daniell. He was an Alaskan expert sailor whom, during the previous year, taught us the intricacies of Alaskan navigation not to be found in any Academy nautical training manual. He was my 'Sea Daddy.'" It was this training in Alaskan navigation that facilitated our rapid, low-visibility, transit through the Aleutian chain. It is now not surprising we all became successful career Coast Guard senior leaders. I'm not sure that any other cutter produced so many future senior leaders at the same time. We may not have known it at the time, but we were truly the A-Team.

We operated with the philosophy you train as you do and do as you train. In the month leading up to the crash, we routinely trained with our embarked AVDET in refueling, takeoffs, landings, LSO and HCO qualifications, and, most importantly, low-visibility landing approaches. During the initial hectic time of uncertainty, we relied on our training to prosecute that case with a quiet self-confidence.

I would be remiss if I did not also mention two other *Mellon* senior enlisted leaders: Quartermaster Chief (QMC) Simokat, and Radarman Chief (RDC) Beckham. Chiefs Simokat and Beckham also were very recent graduates of the National Search and Rescue School. Chief Beckham was by far the best Shipboard Landing approach controller with whom I've had the pleasure of sailing. Having three recent National SAR school graduates aboard one cutter was unusual for a cutter in the early 1980s. Between Chiefs Simokat and Beckham and myself, we manned *Mellon's* CIC as On Scene Commander continuously during the period of this recuse case. Our recent formal Rescue training coupled with the dedication and professionalism of both chiefs was instrumental in the successful outcome of this operation. Our recent formal SAR training facilitated our successful planning and coordination efforts of Air Force, Navy, and Coast Guard Forces.

I often wonder what brought all of these unique factors together at the same time. Why was *Mellon* near Attu in the first place, because I asked Marty Daniell to visit Attu, a station I had previously commanded? This visit provided area familiarity with the geography as well as face-to-face contact with Attu personnel, which would prove extremely beneficial during the operation. Why were Bill Peterson and Mike Wallace the assigned AVDET? After serving nearly 11 years on flight deck-equipped cutters, Bill and Mike were by far two of the three best and most gifted aviators with whom I had ever served. Additionally, Bill's Sea Daddy was also Marty Daniell. Not only was he Daniell-trained, but Admiral Daniell knew his personality extremely well. Missy Wall, Dee Parker, Bill Peterson, Mike Wallace, and I all became senior Coast Guard leaders.

We were the best people for this rescue, with the best training for this mission, with the best leadership for this operation. Fate, luck, or divine intervention: someone was looking out for those survivors. The Coast Guard is, however, Always Ready...*Semper Paratus*. It is staffed with personnel who will 'always' demonstrate Honor, Respect, Devotion to Duty, and Courage."[78]

ENS/01 Dee Parker (now Dee Norton) was *Mellon's* Communications Officer, Deck Watch Officer, and HCO. ENS Parker came to *Mellon* after completing Officer Candidate School in Yorktown, Virginia (Class 6-80). This was her first assignment in the Coast Guard. Before this, she recently had graduated with a degree in law enforcement from Northern Arizona University.

ENS Parker rose to the rank of Captain (CAPT/06). She served as Executive Officer at Base Galveston, Operations Officer at Group Miami, and Commander of Coast Guard Group Honolulu. She also served in several staff positions in support of Coast Guard personnel. CAPT Norton retired after 25 years in the Coast Guard and currently works as the Special Assistant to the Deputy Assistant Director for Immigration and Customs Enforcement (ICE) Air Operations in Mesa, Arizona.

"Looking back on the events on the rescue of CG-1600," she said, "it seems like eons ago this occurred but on the other hand, parts are very vivid and they are still fresh in my mind. I was a qualified Deck Watch Officer and also the Communications Officer for *Mellon*, but I had little time on board when this occurred. Another duty I performed was Helicopter Control Officer (HCO). In this position I would talk to the pilots and work with them on their landings, takeoffs, and general communication when they were in flight. I actually had quite a bit of training as the HCO because we spent days at a time working with the flight crews from Air Station Port Angeles when they were performing touch-and-go landings.

I remember we were in the vicinity of Attu, which was unusual for an Alaskan Patrol. When the call came in that the plane was missing and overdue, all crewmembers came together and worked as a team to get ready for the search and rescue operation. As Communications Officer, I worked with my Senior Chief Radioman (RMCS) and his RMs to ensure the message traffic was complete and up to date. Additionally, since the rescue also involved other Coast Guard units and Air Force and Navy assets, communications were key to keeping the message traffic flowing with accurate information. Initially I spent a lot of time on working communica-tions with all parties involved.

This evolution took quite a bit of time. The QMC and RDC worked diligently to plan out search plans for *Mellon*. Eventually *Mellon* deployed small boat crews to send ashore to begin searching for the missing seaman. I had requested to be part of the teams that went ashore but was told I was needed on the bridge as HCO. So I spent a lot of my time on the bridge talking to the various search and rescue aircraft participating in this operation. I also remained double-hatted as the Communications Officer and ensured Captain Daniell and LT Sabo were kept up to date on the message traffic. The time spent on the bridge was stressful, but I felt it was so worthwhile, and, when the plane was found, all on the bridge were extremely elated.

After this, the rescue part of the mission kicked in, and working with Shemya AFB in the Aleutian Islands was a bit challenging. The Coast Guard cutters did not normally operate in their vicinity because of the secure environment. In this instance, the Air Force worked closely with the Coast Guard to ensure the survivors from - CG-1600 were taken care of and transferred to the appropriate medical facility.

Although a relatively new officer in the Coast Guard, I was truly impressed by the professionalism displayed by the senior leadership and the crew in this mission. I know the helicopter crews were sorely fatigued, but they did not stop searching. All pulled together. Maybe this incident made the positive impression on me of just what the Coast Guard was capable of. Later I attended the National Search and Rescue School, and this case was discussed in my training as one that went well. CAPT Daniell and LT Sabo were both proactive and supportive of all junior officers. Their faith and trust in me assisted me in my duties during this evolution."[79]

ENS Missy Wall rose to the rank of Commander (CDR/O5). Missy was impressed with ship-helicopter operations and the HH-

52 mission in ALPAT. She applied to flight school after this deployment and was selected, only to be medically disqualified when she blew out her knee in a skiing accident celebrating her selection to flight school! She became the CO of LORAN Station St. Paul and *Farallon* (WPB-1301). CDR Wall served as executive officer of *Courageous* (WHEC-622) and Group Miami FL. She retired after 20 years of service.

"It was a real test for everyone and an incredible rescue," she said. "My single biggest lesson learned from that long day would be the loneliness of a tough command decision. Yes, everyone thought CAPT Daniell would say "Go" after the briefing, but he didn't and he couldn't. It was outside the bounds of the level of risk to which he could subject his aircrew. I would live that lesson many times over in my career. My crew didn't need to agree with me, but I wanted them to understand why I did what I did. CAPT Daniell was a mentor and role model throughout my career. I hold him in the highest esteem and regard. The entire crew of Mellon did. A crew that gives you a flawless 9-minute helicopter refuel operation when lives were on the line is nothing short of remarkable. That effort would become the gold standard I'd try to achieve with my crews. For a young boot ensign, to be even a small part of such a well-oiled machine was a great experience that left me wanting to do and to be more in the Coast Guard." [80]

Rescue-1425

Smitty, Wally, and I received the prestigious Association of Naval Aviation (ANA) Helicopter Crew of the Year Award for 1982 for the rescue. Secretary of the Navy, the Honorable John F. Leman, was present when Coast Guard RADM W.B. Kozlowsky presented the award to us at the ANA Symposium awards luncheon, in Norfolk, VA.

Smitty was awarded the Air Medal for his outstanding efforts hoisting, assisting in the helicopter's safe navigation, preparing the survivors for extraction, and maintaining the helicopter throughout the rescue. Smitty was promoted to petty officer first class (AM1/E6) and transferred to CGAS Port Angeles in the fall of 1982. Smitty retired from the Coast Guard after more than 20 years of distinguished service.

Wally was awarded the Meritorious Service Medal for his exceptionally meritorious service while acting as copilot and senior ground party member. Wally was cited for outstanding efforts in aerial flight; providing first aide and coordinating the evacuation of the four survivors suffering from severe injuries and hypothermia; and staying at the crash site to lead the search efforts for the missing crewman. Wally continued his Coast Guard career, transferring to CGAS Cape Cod near his home town of Cambridge, MA. In 1985, flying the HH-3F Pelican, he was awarded the Distinguished Flying Cross for rescuing two people who crashed their plane into the White Mountains of New Hampshire on December 3, 1985. Battling 100-knot gusting winds, severe turbulence, and blowing snow, he was able to hoist the survivors to safety. In 1985, for the second time, he earned the ANA Award for Helicopter Crew of the Year for their rescue of six mariners from a fishing vessel that sank in poor weather 150 miles off the coast of Cape Cod. He became the only Coast Guard, Navy, or Marine Corps pilot to received that prestigious award twice.

Wally was chosen to be the Operations Officer for CGAS Sitka in 1993. In 1996 he was selected as the CO for CGAS Brooklyn, NY. After his successful tour as CO, Wally was promoted to Captain (CAPT/06) and was assigned Coast Guard District Eleven in Alameda, CA, as Chief of Search and Rescue. Wally was transferred to Washington DC, where he completed his 31-year career working as the Coast Guard Liaison Officer to the Department of State and the Deputy to the Assistant Commandant for Acquisitions in 2007.

I was awarded the Distinguished Flying Cross for extraordinary achievement in aerial flight during the rescue. I continued my operational career in the Coast Guard, serving next as a HH-52 and HH-65 instructor pilot and flight examiner, and ship/helo instructor at the CG Aviation Training Center in Mobile, AL. I returned to Kodiak as Operations Officer from 1993 to 1996. I served as CO of CGAS New Orleans (1996 to 1998) and Group/Air Station Port Angeles, WA (2001 to 2004). I held staff positions at Coast Guard Headquarters in Washington DC in the Aviation Plans, Programs, and Budgeting Branch (1991 to 1993) and Coast Guard District Thirteen in Seattle, WA, as Chief of

Search and Rescue Branch and then Acting Chief of Operations (1998 to 2001). I retired from the Coast Guard in December 2005 as the Chief of Aviation Forces at Coast Guard Headquarters in Washington DC after logging more than 4,000 flight hours in rescue helicopters.

CGAS Kodiak Rescue-1602

CDR Jim Wright was on his second operational tour, as Operations Officer, at CGAS Kodiak when the mishap occurred. It was unprecedented in Coast Guard aviation history that a HC-130H would sustain strike damage on the side of a mountain. Under CDR Wright's leadership, CGAS Kodiak recovered with a renewed sense for flight safety, crew coordination, and mission risk. Many of his policies and programmatic updates were still in effect when I took over as Operations Officer in 1993. To this day, CDR Wright remembers the radio dialog with Rescue-1425.

"How powerless I felt as the helicopter inched its way up the side of the mountain in the fog, rain, and wind to the survivors. We on the C-130 vividly could imagine that the helo crew was acting more like an ATV than a rotary wing aircraft, without the benefit of wheels on the ground. This was the most complex and remote a SAR case I have ever been associated with in my 20 years in the Coast Guard. We had so many people doing selfless work...AVDET, *Mellon*, LORAN Station, Shemya AFB, and other CGAS Kodiak crews. Seeing the photos of wreckage and knowing how bad the weather was, I was totally astounded that we had survivors."

CDR Wright served 20 years in the Coast Guard, retiring as CO of Air Station Traverse City MI in 1985. CDR Wright logged more than 5,400 flight hours in Coast Guard aircraft and another 11,000 hours as a commercial airline pilot. Wright retired from United Air Lines in 2003.[81]

LCDR Kyle Jones had the distinction of being the only person at CGAS Kodiak that participated both in flying on the rescue and as a member of the MAB. Jones flew an additional 20.5 flight hours to ferry the MAB and Investigation Board to and from Anchorage and Attu. Jones served 30 years in the military, four in the Marines and 26 in the Coast Guard, rising to the rank of Captain (CAPT/0-6). He continued to fly operationally after CGAS Kodiak, logging a total of 9,700 flight hours in various Coast Guard aircraft (HH-52, HH-3, HU-16, HC-130s, and HU-25). He participated in nine mishap investigations over his years in Coast Guard aviation.

"The Attu mishap was clearly the most challenging, gut wrenching, emotionally agonizing, and lengthy investigation," he said. "The fact that anyone survived this mishap is amazing."

CAPT Jones retired from the Coast Guard in 1996 and flew as a commercial pilot for NetJets until 2010, logging another 10,000 flight hours. He continues to fly for the Coast Guard with his Bonanza V-35 in the Coast Guard Air Auxiliary.[82]

CGAS Kodiak

The Coast Guard Support Center Kodiak Chapel bulletin for Sunday 8 August 1982 read:

> *Dear Parish Family,*
> *Last Friday July 30th was a beautiful day! Yes, I know it started raining about 0530, but as I'm told- "Kodiak people are adaptable." Consequently plan #2 was initiated. My house was warmed from a distance. With the spirit of love and interest being as beautiful and strong as it was, I can easily understand how that could happen.*
> *Fr. Richard*
> *MASS IN THANKSGIVING- Today our parish Mass will be a mass in Thanksgiving! Let's join together and thank God for the miracles of Friday July 30. The miracle for the crew of the C-130 and their families, and the miracle that God worked through the heroism of the helo crew- LT W. Peterson, LT M. Wallace, and AM2 Smith. How good is God in his love in the people and friends around us! Let's include in the Mass the miracle of the crews who "back up" and stand ready, who serve and keep all those ships and planes up to their missions to rescue and serve others, and especially the crew- those special persons the wives and family of those who "go out!"*

Was it all a coincidence? Nine survived the crash on the mountain at Attu. CG-1600's Emergency Locating Beacon was not working, and, two hours after the crash, a working Emergency Beacon was found and energized from a survival vest that had not burned. *Mellon* with her deployed AVDET was within 150 nm of the crash site when they could have been anywhere in the Alaskan exclusive economic zone (EEZ), which is the size of one half the continental United States. *Mellon's* crew was trained and skilled enough to transit at high speed on turbines through hazardous waters in demanding weather conditions and sea states. They performed flawlessly in landing, refueling, and taking off Rescue-1425 in nine minutes. Rescue-1425 and crew were able to negotiate all the hazards and obstacles thrown at us to safely rescue the survivors of CG-1600 in the remotest of locations. Rescue-1602 was airborne on a mission that had cut the distance to Attu from Kodiak in half for its timely divert. Medevac personnel and aircraft made it safely to Shemya from both Kodiak and Fairbanks AK in a timely fashion in poor weather. LORAN Station Attu and Shemya Air Force personnel at Attu for rest and relaxation were fit and able to assist on the rescue in a myriad of ways. Shemya AFB and crew were able to assist with medical and support personnel throughout the rescue.

Miracle comes from the Latin word for wonder and means "a sight to behold." Miracles in the biblical sense require divine intervention. The merely remarkable, improbable, or, in today's parlance "awesome," is not enough to qualify. A true miracle by definition is a supernatural phenomenon.[83]

The Merriam-Webster Dictionary defines providence as divine guidance or care; God conceived as the power sustaining and guiding human destiny.[84]

That dictionary defines coincidence as a situation in which events happen at the same time in a way that is not planned or expected.[85]

Was it a "miracle" or was it "providence" that the crew of CG-1600 was rescued? Was it just a matter of "coincidence"? You, the reader, will have to decide.

However you want to define the rescue, the fact is these young Coast Guard survivors were rescued in one of the remotest and environmentally challenging locations in the United States. They defied all odds in living through the crash and have made the most of lives amidst the myriad of challenges that stood before them.

The End!

CAPT Daniell winging LTJG Peterson in 1979. Peterson collection.

CGAS Kodiak Awards Ceremony (AD3 Hissom, AT3 Jordan, AM3 Hassinger, LT Wallace, LT Peterson missing AM2 Smith who had transferred before the ceremony). Peterson collection.

ANA Award Ceremony in Norfolk VA. Peterson collection.

Afterword

Attu

Attu Island (52-54N Latitude and 172-54.5 E Longitude) is the westernmost point of the Aleutian Islands of Alaska and the United States. Attu is 1,282 nm southwest of Anchorage, AK. The island was purchased as part of "Seward's Folly" when the United States Secretary of State William Seward signed the treaty with Russia for the purchase of Alaska for $7 million dollars on 30 March 1867. Attu is one of the larger Aleutian Islands measuring 35 miles long and 20 miles wide with mountains rising to 3,000 feet.[86]

Attu is known for its dreadful weather conditions and remoteness. "America's most isolated parcel of land" Etta Jones, a government teacher for the Commissioner of Indian Affairs described it in the early 1940s, "a cold, dense, impenetrable fog soaks the island. Howling winds and piercing cold make the island's environment inhospitable, if not forbidding to most. Severe storms can suddenly usher in violent winds that cause rain and snow to blow horizontally. During stormy weather, williwaws-very strong blasts of wind that sweep down from the hills and lift the water up off the surface of the bay-often occur. Storms can last for days. In winter, the spongy tundra becomes slick, frozen muck. Fifty foot waves are not uncommon, and reefs offshore make navigation treacherous."[87]

Etta and her husband Foster Jones lived with 45 native Aleuts in a small village situated around Chichagof Harbor on the eastern side of the island. In August 1941, the Coast Guard cutter *Atlanta* transported the Jones from Dutch Harbor Unalaska to Attu because no passenger vessels served Attu. In the 1940s the Aleuts on Attu had created a self-sufficient village and lived off the sea and land. They fished and hunted for everything they ate except some staples that they purchased from fur traders who came every year to purchase the blue fox furs they trapped. The village pooled all their furs and divided the income among all the members of the village, with a higher share to the trappers.[88]

Attu's worth is mainly its strategic location at the westernmost point of land where the North Pacific Ocean and the Bering Sea meet. Attu is in near both the Russian Kamchatka Peninsula and Japanese Kurile Islands. The Japanese had thought that Doolittle's raiders, who bombed Tokyo on 18 April 1942, could have taken off from a field in the western Aleutians because it was only 1,746 nm from Attu to Tokyo.

In June 1942, Vice Admiral Boshiro Hosogaya and Rear Admiral Kakuji Kakuta would lead the Japanese attack on the American Aleutian Islands. The attack on American soil was three-fold; to create a diversion for Admiral Isoroku Yamamoto's attack at Midway, to draw out and trap the rest of the Pacific Naval fleet, and to secure the Aleutians and protect the Japanese homeland from any further land-based bomber attacks. The plan called for the occupation of Adak, Kiska, and Attu Islands.[89]

On 3 June 1942, the first wave of carrier-based Japanese aircraft bombed and strafed Dutch Harbor and Fort Mears on Unalaska. The Aleutian weather proved more powerful than any man or machine. Both Japanese and American aircraft could not find their targets during the next several days. The Japanese altered their plans when the Battle of Midway and Dutch Harbor did not go as planned. VADM Yamamoto would bypass Adak to land the Japanese occupying forces on Kiska and Attu.[90]

On Sunday morning, 7 June 1942, the Japanese landed troops in Holtz Bay and later in the day attacked the village of Attu in Chichagof Harbor. They attacked from the mountains to the north as the villagers were returning to their homes from church. The villagers ran to their homes as the Japanese soldiers fired at will on their homes. Foster Jones, who had a short-wave radio on which he transmitted weather to Dutch Harbor, transmitted only 4 words: "The Japs are here" before he destroyed the short-wave radio and all letters and reports he had in their home.[91]

The Aleuts of Attu were very personable people, but they hated the Japanese because Japanese marauders had come in the past, stealing their prized fox pelts and killing hunting parties. Caught by surprise, no one fired on the Japanese soldiers. Every villager was ordered from their homes as the Japanese searched and pillaged their homes. The Japanese read a Proclamation to the villagers; it said that they were being rescued from the tyranny and exploitation of the Americans by the Japanese.

Foster Jones became the first causality on 8 June after he did not reveal any information about his short-wave radio transmissions during an interrogation. He was shot in the head and beheaded in front of his wife Etta. Etta Jones was taken as a prisoner of war and interrogated about her husband's work. The Japanese thought he was transmitting information to the U.S Navy or the Russians on Kamchatka. Etta never revealed anything to the Japanese except that Foster had transmitted four words "The Japs are here." She was taken to Japan and interned with Australian nurses who were captured from a hospital in Papua New Guinea. They suffered horrific conditions until freed on 31 August 1945 when U.S Forces rescued them.[6]

The Aleuts from Attu were also taken as prisoners of war to Japan in September 1942 to the island of Hokkaido. They also suffered horrific conditions and food deprivation; only 19 of 45 survived. Hoping to be returned to Attu after the war, they were informed by the U.S. government that there were too few to rebuild their village, which had been burned and destroyed by the Japanese. They were offered transport to begin again in the native village on Atka Island. Some elected not to go to Atka because the Atka Aleuts spoke a different native dialect and were rivals of the Attu villagers.[92]

It was almost a year later in 1943 that U.S. forces undertook "Operation Landcrab" to regain control of Attu and Kiska Islands. The War Department assigned the Army's 7th Motorized Division with 10,000 personnel under the command of Major General Brown, because they were ready for deployment and not needed in North Africa where they were initially headed. The Alaskan Command under the command of Major General Buckner did not have enough personnel to conduct the mission and maintain the defense of Alaska. General Buckner did, however, provide advisors, logistical support, and his 4th Infantry Regiment in combat-ready reserve.

The battle of Attu was an infantry battle. The island was shrouded in fog and swept by high winds every day, making air support very limited. However, the naval presence was vast with three battleships (*Nevada, Idaho, and Pennsylvania*), six cruisers, nineteen destroyers, the escort carrier *Nassau*, and two submarines. The terrain on Attu is steep, with jagged crags, knifelike ridges, and boggy tundra, which made impracticable any extensive use of mechanized equipment. Motor vehicles, even those with treads, would churn the tundra into a muddy mass, sinking treads and wheels and causing them to spin uselessly. The tundra and terrain proved just as difficult for foot soldiers. The constant precipitation allowed water to seep under the muskeg-like moss and coarse grass, and soldiers walking on it would readily break through the tundra to sink in watery mud up to their knees.

A force of 2,600 Japanese troops was dug in when the Battle of Attu began on 11 May 1943. Holtz and Massacre Bays were the main landing and staging locations for the 7th Division. Of the 93 landing craft used in the 20-day battle, only 3 remained operational because reefs, shoals, fog, high winds, and surf sank all the others.[93]

The Battle of Attu was the second-most costly in the Pacific Theater (Iwo Jima the worst). U.S. forces suffered 3,829 casualties: 549 dead; 1,148 wounded; 1,200 severe cold injuries (e.g., frostbite, hypothermia, trenchfoot); 614 disease; 318 other causalities (e.g., accidents, drownings, self-inflicted wounds, and psychiatric break downs), and the Japanese forces suffered complete annihilation with 2,572 dead and only 28 prisoners as 500 of the Japanese soldiers, both wounded and able bodied, committed suicide in lieu of being taken prisoner.[94]

After the battle for Attu was won U.S. forces occupied the island and quickly started building a runway near Alexia Point on the east side of Massacre Bay. By 8 June 8, the airfield was operational, and a submarine base followed. Attu airfield along with a newly constructed airfield at Shemya would be used for the planned invasion of Japan.

Recognizing the tactical importance of Attu and needing enhanced navigational aids for allied ships and aircraft, the first LORAN Station began construction in 1943 at Theodore Point at the western end of Temnac Bay. It became operational in 1944. LORAN Station Attu provided critical navigational information for all vessels and aircraft operating north of Japan in the Pacific.

Information on the LORAN system and all LORAN Stations were classified SECRET during World War II. When the war was over, LORAN was declassified and the navigational system opened for use by all mariners and pilots operating vessels and planes with installed receivers.

In 1949, the LORAN Station was moved to Murder Point, where it remained operational until 1961. In 1961, the station was moved to its final location at Casco Cove adjacent to the new runway. The station was operational until 2010, when it was decommissioned because GPS made LORAN obsolete.[95]

No one permanently lives on Attu now that the Coast Guard has left the island. To view the crash site on Goggle Earth, use the following coordinates: 52-47.5 N 173-07.9 E. Note that high winds pushed the empennage (tail section) down the steep slope approximately 100 yards from its original crash position 2 years after the accident.

Brief History of the Coast Guard in Alaska

The U.S Lighthouse Service and Revenue Cutter Service, predecessors of the U.S. Coast Guard, provided extraordinary assistance to mariners and the government in the late 1800s and early 1900s in the Alaskan waters of the North Pacific and Bering Sea. After the purchase of Alaska by Secretary of State Seward, the Revenue Cutter *Lincoln* was sent with officials from Washington to tour the vast new territory of Alaska. Revenue Cutters began the Bering Sea Patrols in the spring of every year and returned to their homeports in the fall. The cutters provided law and order, medical care, and sometimes food in this isolated region of the U.S. Many heroic acts were documented in these early years to save the natives from a smallpox epidemic, feed the natives with reindeer from Russia, rescue trapped whalers frozen in the ice of the Bering Sea, and stave off the collapse of the fur seals of the Pribilof Islands because of over harvesting.[96]

In 1915, the Coast Guard received its present name under an act of Congress signed by President Woodrow Wilson. The act merged the Revenue Cutter Service with the U.S. Life-Saving Service. The same cutters now sailed the waters of the Bering Sea under the guidance of the new Commandant of the Coast Guard, Commodore Ellsworth P. Bertholf.[97]

President Franklin Roosevelt ordered the transfer of the Lighthouse Service to the Coast Guard in 1939. Finally in1946, Congress permanently transferred the Commerce Department's Bureau of Marine Inspection and Navigation to the Coast Guard. Thus, the Coast Guard became the single multi-mission maritime federal agency dedicated to saving life at sea and enforcing the nation's maritime laws. The Coast Guard operated under the Department of Treasury at that time.[98]

During World War II, the Coast Guard transferred to the U.S. Navy from the Department of the Treasury. Coast Guard cutters and personnel served under the U.S Navy throughout all theaters of the war. After the war, the Coast Guard transferred back to the Department of Treasury.[99]

The Coast Guard's legal authority differs from the other four armed services because it operates simultaneously under Title 10 of the U.S. Code and its other organic authorities, such as Titles 6, 14, 19, 33, and 46. Because of its unique legal authorities, the Coast Guard can conduct both military operations and enforce U.S. laws and regulations. The Posse Comitatus Act of 1878 does not apply to the Coast Guard.

The Coast Guard Law Enforcement mission is authorized in 14 USC 2, "The Coast Guard shall enforce or assist in the enforcement of all applicable laws on, under and over the high seas and waters subject to the jurisdiction of the United States." Coast Guard personnel enforce U.S. law in the world's largest EEZ of approximately 3.4 million square miles. In addition, 14 USC 89 provides the authority for U.S. Coast Guard active duty commissioned, warrant, and petty officers to enforce federal law on waters subject to U.S. jurisdiction and in international waters, as well as on all vessels subject to U.S. jurisdiction (including U.S., foreign, and stateless vessels). The Coast Guard's enduring roles are maritime safety, security, and stewardship.[100]

Brief History of Coast Guard Aviation
The establishment of Coast Guard aviation began in early 1915 when Lieutenants Elmer Stone and Norman Hall conceived the use of aircraft for Coast Guard missions. With the support of their CO, Captain Benjamin Chiswell, they were taken on experimental flights out of the Curtiss Flying School in Newport News VA.

Despite the navigational limits of the aircraft the flights were successful and resulted in Stone and five others being assigned to the Naval Aviation Flight School at Pensacola FL in April 1916.[101]

Later in 1916, Congress authorized the establishment of up to ten air stations but no funds were passed in the appropriations bill. On completion of flight school, the Coast Guard pilots were assigned to naval air stations as the U.S entered World War I in April of 1917.

By the end of the war, Coast Guard aviators had been recognized for heroic efforts. In May 1919, LT Stone piloted a Navy Curtiss NC flying boat (**NC-4)** across the Atlantic Ocean. By 1920, the Coast Guard still had not received any appropriations for air stations, however, an attempt was made to use the abandoned Naval Air Station at Morehead City, NC, with borrowed Navy flying boats. The station was disestablished because of the lack of operating funds in July 1921. Finally in 1925 Congress appropriated funds for five Coast Guard aircraft that were flown from Air Stations in Gloucester, MA, and Cape May, NJ, primarily to combat the smuggling of whiskey during Prohibition.[102]

By the 1930s, shipping had moved offshore, and new flying life boats were pressed into service. By 1938, Coast Guard aviation and funding for Air Stations had grown to eight (Salem, MA; Brooklyn, NY; Cape May, NJ; Charleston, SC; Miami, FL; St. Petersburg, FL; Biloxi, MS; Port Angeles, WA; and San Diego, CA). In 1938, the following statics were recorded by Coast Guard aviation: 1,931 persons warned of impending danger; 335 vessels warned of impending danger; 266 persons in peril assisted; 125 medical cases, 10 off which were facilitated by landings in the open sea; 87 disabled vessels located; and 21 navigation obstructions located. Coast Guard aviation was in the beginning stages of what was to become its search and rescue mission. It was also in this time that the cutter and aircraft were married because Grumman JF-2 amphibians were used to extend the patrol areas for the 327-foot cutters off the East Coast, West Coast, and Alaskan waters.[103]

The Coast Guard was transferred to the Navy Department by Executive Order 8929 on 1 November 1941, just before Pearl Harbor was bombed on 7 December 1941. The Coast Guard was singled out to provide anti-submarine patrols from the coastal air stations because of the devastating attacks by German U Boats along the East and Gulf Coast of the U.S. The problem was none of the Coast Guard aircraft were armed for combat or ASW. Existing aircraft were armed to the limit of their capabilities until 52 OS2U-3 Kingfisher aircraft were acquired and outfitted for ASW operations for the Coast Guard by early 1943.

Coast Guard aircraft engaged in 61 bombing attacks on enemy submarines during the war. Coast Guard patrol aircraft were pressed in to search and rescue missions right from the start of the war because of the loss of so many torpedoed vessels. By 1943 the loss of life associated with the increase in military training and over-water operational missions led to the Coast Guard standing up the first Office of Air Sea Rescue. The Joint Chiefs asked the Coast Guard to develop Air Sea Rescue equipment and operational procedures. Because of it experience in Arctic operations and the International Ice Patrol, Coast Guard aviation created Patrol Squadron 6 assigned to Narsarssuak, Greenland, code named Bluie West-One. The Coast Guard flew PBY-5As and, when additional airframes became available, established detachments in Argentia, Newfoundland, and Reykjavik, Iceland to provide air cover for the North Atlantic and Greenland convoys. During a heroic rescue mission to save the crew of a USAF B-17 that crashed on the Greenland ice cap in December 1942, Lieutenant John Pritchard and Radioman Benjamin Bottoms lost their lives flying from the Coast Guard Cutter *Northland* in a J2F Grumman "Duck,"[104]

Coast Guard aviation took on a primary role in the testing of helicopters for the Navy and Coast Guard in 1943 at CGAS Brooklyn, NY, for both ASW and rescue missions. Under the guidance of CDR William Kossler and LCDR Frank Erickson Sikorsky, HNS-1 and HOS-1 helicopters were used to begin the first ship-helo trials aboard the merchant ships *Bunker Hill*, *Daghestan* and, later, on the cutter *Cobb*. Because of the losses of allied ships by enemy submarines, ASW was the primary mission focus.

Dipping sonar was developed, and successful trials were held in 1945 and early in 1946. Development continued because the Navy saw great promise in helicopter ASW operations to protect convoys and fleet vessels. Erickson continued his vision of the helicopter being a primary rescue asset. He was instrumental in the development of a hydraulic rescue hoist for the helicopter, which made the aircraft a true lifesaving machine.[105]

In the mid-1950s, Coast Guard aviation embraced the capabilities and versatility of the hoist-equipped helicopter because of some heroic efforts in 1955 when Coast Guard helicopters rescued more than 300 people during floods in Connecticut and Massachusetts. Later that same year in California, a Coast Guard helicopter with a double crew rescued 138 people in a 12-hour period; however, the Coast Guard only had 28 helicopters in its entire inventory. It would take several years before Congressional appropriations would allow the Coast Guard to fund the acquisition of new state-of-the-art helicopters and fixed wing aircraft.[106]

Coast Guard HH-52As like CG-1425 flew operationally for 26 years, rescuing more than 15,000 people, the most lives saved by a single helicopter type in the world up to that time. The last HH-52A operational flight took place on 12 September 1989. On 14 April 2016 the restored CG-1426, sister aircraft to CG-1425, was dedicated into the Smithsonian National Air and Space Museum's Steven F. Udvar-Hazy Center.[107]

Brief History of Coast Guard Aviation in Alaska

A Coast Guard AVDET was established on Annette Island AK in early 1944, flying a Grumman JRF amphibian. Annette Island, located 25 miles south of Ketchikan AK, had a 10,000-foot runway and a Canadian Forces Fighter Squadron to protect the critical port of Prince Rupert Canada and to defend the Pacific Northwest. The AVDET on Annette Island was eventually moved to Sitka AK many years later in 1977.

In April 1947, a Coast Guard Air Detachment was established at Kodiak Naval Air Station on Woman's Bay. The Detachment was commanded by LT Ben Dameron. The crew of seven pilots and thirty enlisted crew flew and maintained PBY-5A Catalina aircraft. By 1954, the Kodiak PBYs were replaced by the new Grumman UF-1G Albatross.[108]

In 1957, the Kodiak Air Detachment assumed the duties of Kodiak Search and Rescue Coordinator (RCC Kodiak) from Naval Station Kodiak. All pilots assumed collateral duties as RCC

Controllers when not flying. By 1960, Air Detachment Kodiak had grown, with the addition of a C-123B cargo plane and two HUL-1G helicopters. The C-123 was needed to resupply the remote Alaskan LORAN Stations that were now being upgraded and rebuilt from WWII and the helicopters for deployment on Arctic icebreakers and local SAR around Kodiak.[109]

In 1963, Kodiak Air Detachment had grown to 20 officers and 79 enlisted to fly and maintain four HU-16Es, one C-123B, and four Bell H-13 helicopters. Air Detachment Kodiak was designated Air Station Kodiak as a tenant on Naval Base Kodiak in 1964. By 1969, Air Station Kodiak was flying the modern HC-130 and HH-52 aircraft. The three HC-130s replaced the aging HU-16 Albatross, which ended the seaplane era of Coast Guard in Alaska, and two HH-52 helicopters replaced the H-13s.[110]

In 1970, RCC and Air Station Kodiak prosecuted over 400 SAR cases, saving 168 lives, assisting 881, and saving an estimated $39.6M in property. The Naval Station at Kodiak was disestablished in July 1972, and the Coast Guard took over all operations of the base. Air Station Kodiak's responsibilities increased, especially in fisheries enforcement, under the 1976 Magnuson Fisheries Act.[111]

By1982, Air Station Kodiak had grown to six HC-130s, four HH-3F long-range helicopters, and four HH-52 helicopters for ALPAT deployments on flight deck-equipped cutters. Commensurate with the aircraft increases, Air Station Kodiak personnel grew to 357 personnel to staff and support the extensive operations.[112]

T.O. 1H-52A-1

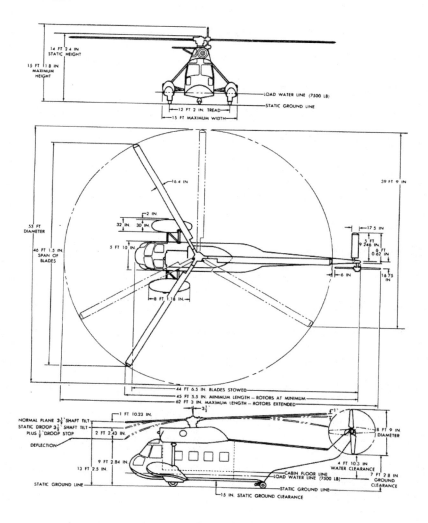

Figure 1-1. Three View Dimensions

HH-52 Three view dimensions. USCG HH-52 Flight Manual.

T.O. 1H-52A-1

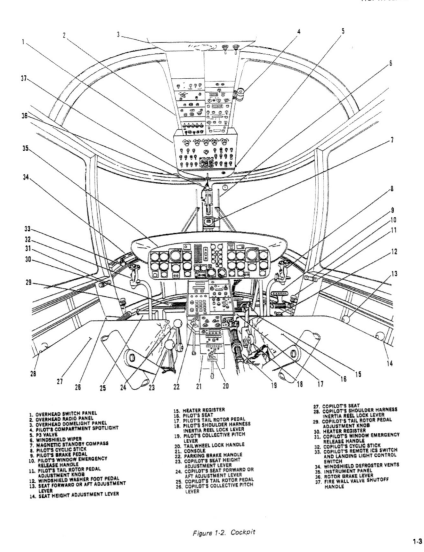

1. OVERHEAD SWITCH PANEL
2. OVERHEAD RADIO PANEL
3. OVERHEAD DOMELIGHT PANEL
4. PILOT'S COMPARTMENT SPOTLIGHT
5. P3 VALVE
6. WINDSHIELD WIPER
7. MAGNETIC STANDBY COMPASS
8. PILOT'S CYCLIC STICK
9. PILOT'S BRAKE PEDAL
10. PILOT'S WINDOW EMERGENCY
    RELEASE HANDLE
11. PILOT'S TAIL ROTOR PEDAL
    ADJUSTMENT KNOB
12. WINDSHIELD WASHER FOOT PEDAL
13. SEAT FORWARD OR AFT ADJUSTMENT
    LEVER
14. SEAT HEIGHT ADJUSTMENT LEVER

15. HEATER REGISTER
16. PILOT'S SEAT
17. PILOT'S TAIL ROTOR PEDAL
18. PILOT'S SHOULDER HARNESS
    INERTIA REEL LOCK LEVER
19. PILOT'S COLLECTIVE PITCH
    LEVER
20. TAIL WHEEL LOCK HANDLE
21. CONSOLE
22. PARKING BRAKE HANDLE
23. COPILOT'S SEAT HEIGHT
    ADJUSTMENT LEVER
24. COPILOT'S SEAT FORWARD OR
    AFT ADJUSTMENT LEVER
25. COPILOT'S TAIL ROTOR PEDAL
26. COPILOT'S COLLECTIVE PITCH
    LEVER

27. COPILOT'S SEAT
28. COPILOT'S SHOULDER HARNESS
    INERTIA REEL LOCK LEVER
29. COPILOT'S TAIL ROTOR PEDAL
    ADJUSTMENT KNOB
30. HEATER REGISTER
31. COPILOT'S WINDOW EMERGENCY
    RELEASE HANDLE
32. COPILOT'S CYCLIC STICK
33. COPILOT'S REMOTE ICS SWITCH
    AND LANDING LIGHT CONTROL
    SWITCH
34. WINDSHIELD DEFROSTER VENTS
35. INSTRUMENT PANEL
36. ROTOR BRAKE LEVER
37. FIRE WALL VALVE SHUTOFF
    HANDLE

Figure 1-2. Cockpit

1-3

HH-52 Cockpit configuration. USCG HH-52 Flight Manual.

HH-52 full autorotation to the water CGAS Port Angeles Stan Visit.
Peterson collection.

CG-1425 secured for sea on *Mellon* ALPAT. Peterson collection.

HH-52 secured for sea on winter ALPAT. Wallace collection.

Acknowledgements

I would like to acknowledge all the outstanding men and women with whom I served in the Coast Guard. Without their unwavering service, rescues such as this would never occur. A "BZ" to CAPT Joe Deer, CAPT Mark Morin, CAPT Jeff Hartman (ret), LT Adam Mullins, BMCM Deane Smith, Dr. David Rosen, Ms. Cathie Zimmerman, and Ms. Nora Chidlow of the Coast Guard for their assistance in obtaining copies of Coast Guard logs, investigations, pictures, and background information.

Many thanks to Dr. Dennis Noble and LCDR Tom Beard (USCG ret) for their guidance and sage advice to assist me in this endeavor. To my fellow workmates at PNNL (Jim, Lee, Tony, Robert, Gordon, and Tim) appreciate your inputs and putting up with the retired guy asking for reviews. To Darlene, Jim, Lance, Phil, John, CZ, and Tom many thanks for your encouragement, inputs, and keeping me focused. My highest praise to Regina for your tremendous assistance in taking my words and transforming them into a real book with sentence structure, punctuation, and formatting.

Appreciate all the inputs and memories from the *Mellon* crew (VADM Martin Daniell, CAPT Jim Sabo, CAPT Dee Norton-Parker, and CDR Missy Wall) as the rescue would not have happened without your leadership and professionalism. Your interviews and inputs were key to telling the story.

A special thanks to those survivors of CG-1600 who provided me interviews and updates on their lives 33 years after the mishap. What a story you have to tell!

Another "BZ" to my good friend and copilot, CAPT Mike Wallace. Wally filled in the blanks on what happened on the side of mountain during the rescue. Wally is "one in a million"-a great friend/brother and one of the best pilot's I have ever flown with. His inputs were critical to the book.

It has been a real journey for me and without the support of my bride, Sue, it could not have happened...the constant late nights on research and middle of the night "ideas" that popped into my head and bolted me out of bed to the office for hours of typing. This work has taken me many years to research and corroborate all the information. After the interviews with the survivors I knew I had to leave my comfort zone and tell the story. It became an obsession to get it all written, then rewritten, rewritten again...in the quest of hopefully a well written book. I am blessed with good family and friends who supported me. Hopefully this book will be educational as well as enjoyable to read. Many thanks to everyone.

About the Authors

CAPTAIN Bill Peterson- Peterson graduated from Vanden High School Travis AFB, CA, in 1972. He entered the U.S. Coast Guard Academy graduated in 1976 with a Bachelor of Science Degree focused on marine science and ocean engineering. Peterson was winged a Naval Aviator in 1979 and is designated Coast Guard Aviator number 1953. Peterson retired from active duty as Chief of Aviation Forces for the Coast Guard in late 2005. Peterson has two grown sons. His oldest is a Federal Parole Officer and National Guard Officer. His youngest is an Immigration and Customs Enforcement Agent and Naval Reserve Corpsman. He is married to Susan (Albright) Peterson and combined they have five married children and nine grandchildren to spoil.

CAPT Mike Wallace- Wallace graduated from Cambridge High and Latin High School in Cambridge, MA, in 1970. He then graduated from North Adams State College, North Adams, MA, in 1975, majoring in biology with a minor in chemistry. He earned his Emergency Medical Technician certification in May 1976, married in June, and then entered and graduated from Coast Guard Officer Candidate School in December 1976. Wallace was winged a Naval Aviator in 1977 and is designated Coast Guard Aviator number 1883. Wallace retired from active duty after 31 years of service in 2007. Wallace has been blessed with the love and support of his wife Sharon, for more than 40 years, and they are both very proud of their family: daughters Meghan and Michelle and granddaughters Emily and Sophia.

Book Insights

VADM Martin Daniell, Commanding Officer of CGC *Mellon*- "This case was a challenge unique in my experience... A critical part of this was landing the helicopter with a load of injured and refueling it in record time for its further transit to Shemya for medical treatment. Alaska and particularly the Western Aleutian Islands pose a unique operating environment. There are virtually no navigational aids, charts are unreliable, and the weather is consistently challenging. That this case had an unquestionably positive outcome is a tribute to the skill of the helicopter crew and to the teamwork of the *Mellon* crew who supported them. I am proud to have been a part of this all-hands effort."

CDR Missy Wall, CGC *Mellon* Helicopter Control Officer- "It was a real test for everyone and an incredible rescue. My single biggest lesson learned from that long day would be the loneliness of a tough command decision. Yes, everyone thought CAPT Daniell would say "Go" after the (second) briefing, but he didn't and he couldn't. It was outside the bounds of the level of risk to which he could subject his aircrew. I would live that lesson many times over in my career...CAPT Daniell was a mentor and role model throughout my career. I hold him in the highest esteem and regard. The entire crew of Mellon did. A crew that gives you a flawless 9-minute helicopter refuel operation when lives were on the line is nothing short of remarkable. That effort would become the gold standard I'd try to achieve with my crews. For a young boot ensign, to be even a small part of such a well-oiled machine was a great experience that left me wanting to do and to be more in the Coast Guard."

Ms. Cathie Zimmerman-Deputy Chief USCG Flight Safety- Be prepared as you are transported back in time to a cold isolated mountain on Attu for a truly remarkable rescue. A must read, you will see the many perspectives of the rescue from the survivors, *Mellon*, LORAN Station, Rescue-1602, and Rescue-1425. Bill does an amazing job of pulling together information from all the investigations and interviews to bring the event to life. His writing is so vivid; it is like you are right on scene as the rescue unfolds. I felt the cold and sweat of Wally and Smitty as they tried to comfort and prepare the survivors for the trek down the mountain. I found myself trying to lift my legs as if I was trying to slug through the spongy soggy tundra as they climbed up and down the mountain. I identified with the helpless feeling Rescue-1602 had as they circled at altitude and listened to Rescue-1425's transmissions. At the same time, Bill makes you understand how reassuring and important it was to have Rescue-1602 overhead; "Big brother looking out for you". I often felt the need to wipe sweat from my brow as Bill fought to keep the helo upright and fly straight and level. As an aviation safety nerd, I found myself several times screaming at the pages "Bill! Oh no, you didn't!" and there are the moments of levity that you just can't help but chuckle. I worked with Bill over the course of my 27 years at CG Headquarters in my aviation safety job and this book captures his passion and enthusiasm for Coast Guard Aviation.

Endnotes

[1] "United States Coast Guard Search and Rescue Summary Statistics 1964 thru 2013", U.S. Coast Guard. https://www.uscg.mil/hq/cg5/cg534/SARfactsInfo/SAR%20Sum%20Stats%2064-13.pdf., accessed 8/1/16.

[2] "USCGC *Mellon* (WHEC 717)," U.S. Coast Guard. https://www.uscg.mil/pacarea/cgcMellon/, accessed 7/29/16.

[3] "Hypothermia Kills: These Tips Can Save Your Life," U.S. Coast Guard Great Lakes, 9th Coast Guard District. http://greatlakes.coastguard.dodlive.mil/2013/04/hypothermia-kills-these-tips-can-save-your-life/, accessed 7/29/16.

[4] "LORAN Station Attu," LORAN History. http://www.loran-history.info/Attu/attu.htm, access 7/29/16.

[5] "Sikorsky HH-52A Seaguard," U.S. Coast Guard. www.uscg.mil/history/aviation/Sikorsky/HH52/SikorskyHH52A.pdf, accessed 7/29/16.

[6] "KC-135 Stratotanker," Boeing. http://www.boeing.com/history/products/kc-135-stratotanker.page, accessed 7/29/16.

[7] "KC-135 Stratotanker," Boeing. http://www.boeing.com/history/products/kc-135-stratotanker.page, accessed 7/29/16.

[8] "P-3C Orion Long Range ASW Aircraft," United States Navy Fact Sheet, U.S. Navy. http://www.navy.mil/navydata/fact_display.asp?cid=1100&tid=1400&ct=1, accessed 7/29/16.

[9] Garfield, Brian. 2010. *The Thousand-Mile War: World War II in Alaska and the Aleutians*. University of Alaska Press.

[10] Coast Guard Air Operations Manual, COMDTINST 3710.series U.S. Coast Guard.

[11] Interview and Emails with Missy Wall and author March and April 2016.

[12] Pearcy, Arthur. 1991. *U.S Coast Guard Aircraft Since 1916*. Naval Institute Press.

[13] "HC-130H: Hercules," United States Coast Guard Fact Sheet, U.S. Coast Guard. http://www.uscg.mil/hq/cg7/cg711/c130h.asp, accessed 7/29/16.

[14] Pearcy, Arthur. 1991. *U.S Coast Guard Aircraft Since 1916*. Naval Institute Press.

[15] USCG A/S Kodiak records, CGD 17 Official Press Releases, CG-1600 Mishap Reports. 1982. U.S. Coast Guard.

[16] Ibid.

[17] Ibid.

[18] CG-1600 Mishap Reports. 1982. U.S. Coast Guard.

19 Ibid.
20 Ibid.
21 Ibid.
22 Ibid
23 Ibid.
24 Ibid.
25 Ibid.
26 Ibid.
27 Ibid.
28 Interview and emails with Craig Michals and author March and April 2016.
29 CG-1600 Mishap Reports. 1982. U.S. Coast Guard.
30 Ibid.
31 Interview and emails with Craig Michals and author March and April 2016.
32 CG-1600 Mishap Reports. 1982. U.S. Coast Guard.
33 Interview with Mark Crocker and author 4 February 2016.
34 Interview with Dave Weise and author 19 March 2016.
35 CG-1600 Mishap Reports. 1982. U.S. Coast Guard.
36 Interview with Ken Stevens and author 1 February 2016.
37 CG-1600 Mishap Reports. 1982. U.S. Coast Guard.
38 "Search and Rescue Radio," Green Radio Germany.
http://www.greenradio.de/e_urt33.htm, accessed 7/29/16.
39 CG-1600 Mishap Reports. 1982. U.S. Coast Guard.
40 Ibid.
41 Ibid.
42 "Helicopter Pilots Are Different," Harry Reasoner, ABC News, February 16, 1971. http://www.nixwebs.com/SearchK9/helitac/helicopterpilots.htm, accessed 7/29/16.
43 Shipboard Helicopter Operations Manual, COMDTINST 3710.2 series. U.S. Coast Guard.
44 International Code of Signals for Visual, Sound, and Radio Communications, United States Edition. 1969 as amended. Publication-102, National Imagery and Mapping Agency, Washington, D.C. Available online at http://www.seasources.net/PDF/PUB102.pdf, accessed 8/4/16.
45 Shipboard Helicopter Operations Manual, COMDTINST 3710.2 series. U.S. Coast Guard.
46 Cobra Dane (U)," Federation of American Scientists. http://fas.org/spp/military/program/nssrm/initiatives/cobradan.htm, accessed 7/29/16.
47 Interview and Emails with Dee Parker/Norton and author April and May 2016.
48 CG-1600 Mishap Reports. 1982. U.S. Coast Guard.
49 Ibid.
50 Ibid.
51 Garfield, Brian. 2010. The Thousand-Mile War: World War II in Alaska and the Aleutians. University of Alaska Press.

[52] Baum, Dan, *Anchorage Times,* "Crash survivors receive treatment", Sunday 1 August 1982, Pages A-1 and A-6.

[53] CG-1600 Mishap Reports. 1982. U.S. Coast Guard.

[54] Interview with Mark Whyte and author 15 February 2016.

[55] Baum, Dan, *Anchorage Times,* "Crash survivors receive treatment", Sunday 1 August 1982, Pages A-1 and A-6.

[56] Ibid.

[57] *Kodiak Daily Mirror*, "Weather continues to delay crash probe", Wednesday 4 August 1982, Page 1.

[58] Interview with Mark Whyte and author 15 February 2016.

[59] CG-1600 Mishap Reports. 1982. U.S. Coast Guard.

[60] Ibid.

[61] Interview with Dave Weise and author 19 March 2016.

[62] Interview with Mark Crocker and author 4 February 2016.

[63] Interview and emails with Craig Michals and author March and April 2016.

[64] CG-1600 Mishap Reports. 1982. U.S. Coast Guard.

[65] Interview with Ken Stevens and author 1 February 2016.

[66] "Special Psychiatric Rapid Intervention Team (SPRINT), Naval Medicine. http://www.med.navy.mil/sites/nme/Pages/Psychiatric(SPRINT).aspx, accessed 7/29/16.

[67] Interview with Ken Stevens and author 1 February 2016.

[68] Interview with Mark Whyte and author 15 February 2016.

[69] Interview with Dave Weise and author 19 March 2016.

[70] Ibid.

[71] Interview with Mark Crocker and author 4 February 2016.

[72] Interview and emails with Craig Michals and author March and April 2016.

[73] Christopher Devlin-Young. Homepage. http://www.gocdy.com/, accessed 7/29/16

[74] CG-1600 Mishap Reports. 1982. U.S. Coast Guard

[75] Larkin, VADM C. E. 1982. Meritorious Unit Commendation for the rescue of CG-1600

[76] *CGC Mellon* official ships Logs (redacted) U. S. Coast Guard archives.

[77] Interview and Emails with Martin Daniell and author February and March 2016.

[78] Interview and Emails with Jim Sabo and author March and April 2016.

[79] Interview and Emails with Dee Parker/Norton and author April and May 2016.

[80] Interview and Emails with Missy Wall and author March and April 2016.

[81] Interview and Emails with Jim Wright and author March and April 2016.

[82] Interview and Emails with Kyle Jones and author March and April 2016.

[83] "The Church's Teaching on Miracles," Catholics United for the Faith. http://www.cuf.org/2004/04/above-and-beyond-the-churchs-teaching-on-miracles/, accessed 7/29/16.

84 http://www.merriam-webster.com/dictionary/providence, accessed 7/29/16
85 http://www.merriam-webster.com/dictionary/coincidence, accessed 7/29/16
86 "Aleutian History," Bear Creek. http://www.hlswilliwaw.com/aleutians/Aleutians/html/aleutian-history.htm, accessed 7/29/16.
87 Breu, Mary. 2009. *Last Letters from Attu: The True Story of Etta Jones, Alaska Pioneer and Japanese POW.* Alaska Northwest Books.
88 Ibid.
89 Garfield, Brian. 2010. *The Thousand-Mile War: World War II in Alaska and the Aleutians.* University of Alaska Press.
90 Ibid.
91 Breu, Mary. 2009. *Last Letters from Attu: The True Story of Etta Jones, Alaska Pioneer and Japanese POW.* Alaska Northwest Books.
92 Ibid.
93 Garfield, Brian. 2010. *The Thousand-Mile War: World War II in Alaska and the Aleutians.* University of Alaska Press
94 Ibid.
95 "LORAN Station Attu," LORAN History. http://www.loran-history.info/Attu/attu.htm, accessed 7/29/16.
96 Noble, Dr. Dennis L. 1991. *Alaska and Hawaii: A Brief History of U.S. Coast Guard Operations.* U.S. Coast Guard Historian's Office, available online at https://www.uscg.mil/history/articles/AlaskaHawaii.pdf, accessed 8/1/16.
97 "Commandants of the U.S. Coast Guard and Chiefs of the Revenue Marine Division," U.S. Coast Guard. http://www.uscg.mil/history/faqs/comm.asp, last accessed 8/1/16.
98 "U.S. Coast Guard History," U.S. Coast Guard. http://www.uscg.mil/history/web/USCGbriefhistory.asp, last accessed 8/1/16.
99 Ibid.
100 "Office of Law Enforcement (CG-MLE)," U.S. Coast Guard. http://www.uscg.mil/hq/cg5/cg531/, accessed 8/1/16.
101 "The U.S. Coast Guard Aviation History Timeline 1915 to 2008," U.S. Coast Guard. https://www.uscg.mil/history/aviation/articles/Pteros/CGAviationHistoryIntro.asp, accessed 8/1/16.
102 Ibid.
103 Ibid.
104 Ibid.
105 Ibid.
106 Ibid.
107 *Restored US Coast Guard Helicopter Dedicated at the Smithsonian*, SITREP 2-16 Summer 2016 PTEROGRAM, page 3. Official Publication of the Coast Guard Aviation Association, The Ancient Order of the Pterodactyl.

108 "The U.S. Coast Guard Aviation History Timeline 1915 to 2008," U.S. Coast Guard.
https://www.uscg.mil/history/aviation/articles/Pteros/CGAviationHistoryIntro.asp, accessed 8/1/16.
109 Ibid.
110 Ibid.
111 Ibid.
112 Pearcy, Arthur. 1989. *A History of U.S. Coast Guard Aviation*, Naval Institute Press.

Lightning Source UK Ltd.
Milton Keynes UK
UKOW07f1813151116

287723UK00013B/110/P